THE VICTOR

THE VICTOR

The Victor Landero Story

As told to BOB OWEN
With DAVID M. HOWARD

Fleming H. Revell Company
Old Tappan, New Jersey

All Scripture quotations are based on the King James Version of the Bible.

Library of Congress Cataloging in Publication Data

Landero, Victor.
   The victor.

      1. Landero, Victor. 2. Evangelists—Colombia—
Biography. I. Owen, Bob. II. Howard, David M.
III. Title.
BV3785.L27A38   269'.2'0924[B]   78-26841
ISBN 0-8007-0974-8

Contents

Preface

The first time I met Victor, a slight twinge of disappointment touched me. I don't really know what I expected to see, but I probably anticipated a much more impressive person in outward appearance and personality. For well over a year, I had been hearing about the extraordinary ministry God was giving to him, so I had allowed an image to develop that was my fantasy rather than his reality.

I found a quiet, retiring man. He seemed reticent to speak very much at first. In my years of close association with him, from that time on, I discovered that it took time to get close to him. His humility was so genuine that he honestly felt inferior to other people. He was hesitant to speak out when someone else with whom he was not intimately acquainted was present.

Because he was the first person in his entire area to come to Christ, Victor did not have the privilege of knowing many Christians who were older in the faith than he was. Thus he had little opportunity to be taught by older Christians. The result was that most of what he learned in his early years as a Christian came from his own study of the Bible. Reading was difficult for him, since he had never had formal schooling of any sort. But with what little skill he had in reading, he saturated himself in the Word of God.

When I began visiting Victor in the backwoods, a deep
and growing friendship developed, which I cherish as one
of God's most precious gifts of my entire life.

I had the privilege over a period of years to travel extensively with Victor to the churches which had come into
existence through his witness. As we would walk through
the jungles together or ride on horseback over the hills or
sit for long hours in a dugout canoe gliding down a lazy
tropical river, he would slowly begin to open up. Only
when we had been together for a minimum of two or three
days would he loosen up enough to share the innermost
workings of God in his life. A quick trip of a day or two with
Victor was what he called *visita de medico*—that is, "a doctor's visit." In other words, the "doctor" would rush in,
examine the patient, give a prescription, and be gone again.
Such visits, I soon learned, were not worth the time.

On the other hand, when we were together for a longer
period, he would begin to open his heart. Probably he
thought of me as his teacher. The truth was often quite the
opposite. I am convinced that I learned far more from him
than he ever learned from me. Although I had college and
theological training, and he had never been to first grade,
he was literally my teacher, in a profound way, as he shared
his walk with God and his experiences of the Holy Spirit.

Invariably, after I had been with Victor for an extended
visit in his area, he would make a special point of taking me
aside before I left. Usually he would lead me off into the
woods, where we could sit alone on a log and be undis-
turbed by anyone else. Then he would say something like
this: "Don David, you have now been here with us for some
days. You have observed the work of the Lord in our midst.
You have had opportunity to see where we are in our

spiritual growth. Now, before you go, what is your word
from God for us? What do we need to learn now? What are
the dangers that you see for us? And what word of exhorta-
tion will you leave with us?"

Needless to say, I deeply appreciated such an attitude. It
was the attitude of a true disciple—one who was always
eager to learn more of God and His ways. Those times were
some of the most valuable and memorable experiences of
my life.

Years later, when I wrote a book on the Holy Spirit (*By
the Power of the Holy Spirit*, Inter-Varsity Press) I had no
problem in deciding to whom to dedicate the book. The
dedication reads: "To Victor, Gregorio, Calixto, Maria, and
other Colombians who taught me by their lives what the
fulness of the Holy Spirit means." Much of the content of
that book grew out of our struggles together, as we sought
to understand, in the light of Scripture, what the church in
Colombia was experiencing.

I first wrote about Victor in another book, published in
1969 (*Hammered as Gold*, Harper and Row). However, so
much has happened in the past decade that it seems quite
appropriate that a more complete account of the work of
God in the life of this humble man should now be published. The early years of his Christian experience were
dramatic in their development. Equally important, however, has been his continued faithfulness and growth in the
Lord. Victor was no "flash in the pan." He was no "soaring
rocket" who burned out quickly. Rather he is a quiet,
steady man of God who, like Enoch, has walked with God.
As the Master whom he serves, he has written no books,
founded no cities, led no armies, has never traveled very far
from the spot where he was born. But the impact of this

uneducated yet brilliant man has brought life to hundreds,
indeed thousands, of people. And the ripples which started
in Colombia in his quiet ministry today have become waves
that have literally reached around the world in their influ-
ence.

Victor has now walked with God for over twenty years. In
the summer of 1977 I visited him in the jungles of Colombia, near the border of Panama, where he is attempting to
plant a church among the Indians. We had not seen each
other for ten years. Yet it seemed as if it had been only a
matter of days. Our hearts were immediately knit together
again in love and fellowship. We reminisced about "old
times." We prayed and thanked the Lord together for His
work in our lives. And he told me some of his new experiences as a disciple. When I left, he lamented that our time
together was so short. He said, "There is so much more I
wanted to share with you of what God is doing in my life, of
my struggles to reach these Indians, of the work of the Holy
Spirit."

I am thankful that Bob Owen was also able to visit Victor
and gather material for this book. It has been a privilege for
me to add to that material information from my own notes
and memory so that Bob could weave together this account
of one of God's special servants. The Church around the
world needs to know of men like Victor, who today are
shining examples of the gracious work of the Spirit of God
and of faithfulness to Him in daily walk. My own life has
been forever changed and vastly enriched through my
friendship with Victor. If this book can contribute in some
small way to encouraging others in obedience to the Spirit
of God, Bob Owen and I shall be deeply gratified.

DAVID M. HOWARD

Foreword

It is an undeserved favor—by definition, an "act of grace"—that I have been invited to comment on the extraordinary story of Victor Landero. Actually, my direct, personal acquaintance with him is extremely limited. The only time I had the pleasure of meeting Victor Landero was at a World Vision pastors' conference in Medellín, Colombia. David Howard told me, "There's a man here whom I want you to meet. His story is a remarkable one."

We met. We talked. We opened our hearts to each other. We knew instantly that we were brothers in Christ. When our time of fellowship was over, I knew that I had met a man whose modesty of manner hid a greatness that was quite out of the ordinary. Before the week was finished, I learned much more about Victor Landero. I have since read with eagerness what he and others have written about his new life in Christ and the ministry of love which the Holy Spirit has so powerfully bestowed upon him.

After long years of mingling with Christians in the worldwide family of faith, one learns that God has no time for the carbon-copy business. He specializes in originals—and God's uniqueness of design, as seen in the life and work of Brother Victor, is as fascinating as it is phenomenal.

Here is a man who was deprived of formal training, yet who has been a thirsty learner in the school of Christ. How many promotions he has earned is known only to the Master Himself. What we do know is that he is ablaze with evangelistic fervor and aglow with pastoral concern and compassion. He is both a strategist for the long haul—and a tactician for the immediate task at hand.

Victor Landero is a twentieth-century Barnabas: ". . . full of the Holy Spirit and of faith."

PAUL S. REES

THE VICTOR

1

The New Man

It was noisy in the cantina, but Roberto Urda didn't seem to mind. He was hot and tired, in need of a beer and a woman. And he knew he could obtain both at my cantina. Plunking himself down at a table, Roberto motioned for service. I decided to serve him myself.

I had to speak above the clamor of the guitars and dancers. "Buenos dias, Roberto. What'll you have today?"

"A beer, amigo."

I nodded and turned to get it. "Wait," Roberto said, "bring two beers."

When I brought the drinks, Roberto motioned to a chair. "Join me, Victor.

"Now, Victor—like old times. Two beers. I've paid for them. One for me. One for you."

"No, thanks."

Roberto bristled. "But you *must* drink. You always did. We always drank together."

Again I refused. "Thanks just the same."

"Why won't you drink with me? Aren't we still friends?"

"We are still friends. But I don't drink anymore."

"Don't drink anymore? That's crazy, Victor! I've known

you for a long time. And we've always gotten drunk together. Why? What's the matter?"

"Come by some night, and I'll tell you," I said and left Roberto to drink both his beers. When Roberto left the cantina, some other customers said, "Victor, what's happened to you? Have you become one of the Evangelicals?"

I nodded.

"Did they tell you not to drink?"

"No, but none of them drink."

"But it's bad for your business."

"I can't help it."

A few days later, Roberto came again, and the same scene was repeated, but with a different ending. This time, when I refused to drink the beer, Roberto shoved the glass across the table with such force that beer slopped onto the table.

"Drink it!" Roberto shouted. "I have paid for it. You must drink it with me!"

Again I refused.

Suddenly Roberto leaped to his feet and poured the beer all over my head and face. "There! I bought it for you. Now you've got it!"

Instantly the music stopped, and there was dead silence in the place. I got up slowly, the foamy liquid dripping from my hair. "Thanks, Roberto." Then I deliberately picked up the empty glass and carried it back to the bar. Roberto just stood there, dumbfounded, shaking his head.

"What's happened to Victor?" Roberto asked another customer.

The man shrugged, "*Quíen sabe?* Who knows? He's been different since he got tangled up with the Evangelicals."

"Then it's true? He is an Evangelical himself?"

Another shrug. "*Quíen sabe?*"

Roberto stood looking at me for a long time. Then, shaking his head in bewilderment, he downed the remaining beer and strode out into the street.

Roberto wasn't the first to notice what they called my "strange" behavior. As the owner of the only cantina in the village of Nueva Estación, I was doing all right for myself. I was making plenty of money and living pretty much as I pleased. Then something happened that turned my life around.

It all started several years before that time, with that passing contact with one of the Evangelicals.

When Pedro Gutierrez, one of the Latin America Mission's first workers, had ridden his tired, heavily laden horse into Providencia that day, neither he nor anybody else could have envisioned that his coming would set in motion a chain of events that was to transform the lives of thousands in Colombia. Providencia was a tiny, insignificant village, located barely eight degrees above the equator. It had a reputation as a refuge for outlaws.

As usual, the day was hot and humid. And each plodding footstep of the weary horse whipped little spurts of dust over Pedro's sandaled feet. He was bone weary when he climbed stiffly from the saddle to rest. Later that evening, he preached and offered Bibles for sale.

Selling Bibles might have seemed like a futile effort, because hardly anybody in this entire community could
either read or write.

I happened into town too late to hear the preaching. As I
joined the curious crowd, I saw Pedro hold a book high.
"Only five pesos. . . ."

"What's going on?" I asked one of the bystanders.

"He's selling Bibles, amigo."

"Bibles? What's a Bible?"

"It's a book that tells how God made the world."

I thought that over. "It tells how God made the world?"

"*Si, señor*. Yes, sir."

"I'd like to know how He did that." I rummaged in my
pocket for a tattered bill and pushed my way to the front of
the crowd.

2

The Book With the Answers

For me, Victor Landero, to have purchased a Bible, or any book for that matter, was a miracle. Besides owning and operating the local cantina—consisting of a bar, a brothel, and a dance hall—I could neither read nor write.

I regularly sampled my own wares: drank beer and rum by the quart, slept with my pick of the prostitutes—as well as two other women, one in a nearby village and one on my farm—and danced with the best of them.

All this made me a prime prospect for the message and life-style portrayed in my newly purchased Bible. But, since I couldn't read, I shoved the formidable book into a suitcase and left it there.

"After all," I said to myself, "I only got it because everybody else was buying one." The contents had sounded interesting at the time, but I had more important things to do than to get into the Evangelical's Bible. I just put it away and forgot it.

So, owning that book had absolutely no effect upon my life for several years. Being in business for myself, I gradually learned to read and write, even though I never did go to school. One day I happened to open that old suitcase again. And there it was.

Though I had neglected it, the termites hadn't. As I

checked the book for damage, my curiosity was piqued. I sat down in the midst of my search and began to read.

I read about the Creation, and that was interesting. Then I read a little about this Person Jesus Christ. I couldn't understand much of what I read, but it upset me when I read for the first time that the Jews had killed Jesus. Murdered Him! I was familiar with murder; that kind of violence was common in my country, at that time. But Jesus seemed to have been a good man. Why had they killed Him?

I don't think I was really angry at what they had done to Jesus. I guess it was more compassion than anger.

Anyway, what I read upset me so much that I put the Bible away again. But I couldn't get away from what I had read. Some time after that first reading, I opened the suitcase again, "Just to check on the termite damage," I said to myself.

I didn't realize I was handling dynamite that day when I sat down on a bag of rice in front of my house and began leafing through the pages of the Bible again.

As I sat there, engrossed in my reading, a friend came by and saw me.

"Buenos dias, Victor."

"Buenos dias, Jorge."

"What's that book you are reading?"

"It's a Bible."

"A Bible? Oh, so now you're an Evangelical?"

"An Evangelical? No. I just found this old Bible, and I'm reading it."

Partly to himself and partly to me, Jorge said, "An Evangelical . . . hmm, doesn't add up. Evangelicals don't drink rum, and you still drink rum."

That got my attention. "I'm not an Evangelical. I'm just reading this old Bible."

Jorge nodded, not quite comprehending. He had known me for some time. And what he saw didn't seem to square with my life-style. Jorge walked away, shaking his head.

A few days after that, Eliecer came to town, and my life began to change forever.

Eliecer Benavides had become a Christian several years earlier, through the same man who had sold me my Bible. He had immediately gone to the Caribbean Bible Center in Sincelejo and now was out preaching. Eliecer knew there were no believers in Nueva Estación, which made it a likely target for evangelization.

He thought the best way to begin would be to find somebody with a Bible. But to his knowledge, there was no such person in the village.

Eliecer started his quest in the village plaza. He stopped people one at a time. "Do you own a Bible?" he asked.

A blank look. "A Bible, señor? What is a Bible?"

He'd try another person, ask the same question, and receive the same answer. And so on. A little crowd gathered by this time. And he asked, "Well then, does *anyone* in Nueva Estación own a Bible?"

Silence.

Suddenly Jorge remembered me. He spoke up. "Señor, I know of such a person."

"There is such a person in Nueva Estación? Someone who owns a Bible?"

"Si. And he reads it like an Evangelical."

Eliecer asked, "Who is this man?"

"He lives there," Jorge said, pointing to my house. "His name is Victor Landero."

I had been so busy at the time that I had paid little attention to what was going on, until Eliecer strolled over and introduced himself. He asked about my health, my family, my farm, and my cantina.

After these essentials were out of the way, he asked, "Is it true that you own a Bible?"

"Si," I replied.

"May I see it?"

"Si. . . ." I promptly arose and got the all-important book, not knowing that Eliecer hoped that it, and I, would be the bridge to evangelize this community.

"Do you read this Bible?"

"Si, señor. But it's just a history book. . . ."

Eliecer moved carefully into his punch line. "Victor, this book is more than just an ordinary history book. It's a very unusual book. It's God's Book. It's His holy Word."

My ears pricked up. Suddenly I remembered what the man had said the day I bought the Bible. I asked, "Is it true that this book, the Bible, tells how God made the world?"

Eliecer nodded. "It is true. It tells something more, too. Something even more important."

"Something *more* important? What could that be?"

Eliecer held the book in both his hands. "This book,

amigo, can transform a man's life!"

I caught my breath. Change a man's life? What a startling thing to say. Hidden deep inside, I had a burning desire to change my life. Could it be true that this book was the key? Warily, I asked, "How can this Bible change a man's life?"

Eliecer reverently opened the Bible to the beginning of the New Testament. "Begin reading here," he said. "Read some every day, and it will begin to change your life."

This sounded exciting, intriguing. As soon as Eliecer left, I opened to the Book of Matthew and began reading. But the place I began was dull and uninteresting. I picked it up several times and attempted to wade through it, soon giving up in despair.

I put the Bible aside, not in the suitcase this time, but in the showcase in my store. Unknown to me, this act caused a great deal of speculation and gossip.

My friends and customers began talking. "Victor is an Evangelical now," one would say.

"Victor? An Evangelical? How do you know?"

"The Bible—he reads it very often. And he keeps it where everybody can see it, in the showcase of his store."

"Oh, so Victor *is* an Evangelical. But he still sells rum. How can that be?"

A month or so later, Eliecer returned. He lost no time visiting me. "Buenos dias, Victor. How are you getting along with your reading?"

"It's very dull," I said. "So I lost heart."

"Lost heart, amigo? How can this be?"

"I don't understand anything I read."

"Would you like me to help you understand?"

"Si! Yes, of course. All I read is history. And history is not very interesting."

Eliecer smiled when he realized I had gotten bogged down in the genealogy of Christ. "There is history in the Bible, amigo—of course. But there is much more. Let me show you."

Soon we were deeply engrossed in the Bible. Eliecer flipped the pages with loving familiarity, then handed me the open Bible. "Victor, my brother, read these words— read them aloud."

Haltingly, with a growing awareness, I read, "For all have sinned, and come short of the glory of God."

I stopped, startled. "*All* have sinned? All? Does that mean everybody? Everybody in Nueva Estación?"

Eliecer nodded. "Yes, my friend. Everybody in Nueva Estación. Everybody in all of Colombia. Everybody in the world—*all* have sinned and come short of the glory of God. All."

My heart beat faster as I tried to comprehend the meaning of these words from God's Book. I traced the words again with my finger. "All have sinned. . . ." I took a deep breath.

"That means I'm a sinner?"

It was a question, but those words expressed the anguish of a very sincere, very hungry man. Eliecer knew the feeling. It had come to him, too, not so many years ago. He answered me very gently, with love, "Yes, amigo. God is saying to you, to me, to everybody, that we are sinners."

I sat silently, letting the words penetrate.

"These words are more than history," Eliecer was saying. "They take us all the way back to the beginning of the world—to Adam and Eve. They sinned. All who ever lived since Adam and Eve have sinned. These words bring history right up to the present."

A deep sigh escaped my lips. "All have sinned—all have sinned. I have sinned. And now I'm a sinner. . . ."

Eliecer nodded.

Suddenly I said, "If I am a sinner, what must I do about it?"

Eliecer took a deep breath.

"Amigo," he said, "you have asked the question that Jesus has already answered."

A sense of relief swept through my body. "Jesus has already answered my question?"

"Si, my friend," Eliecer said and leafed through the pages of my Bible again. When he found the place, he said, "Victor, read what Jesus says."

Again, slowly, my body tensed in concentration, my lips sounded out the words, "I tell you . . . except you repent, you shall all . . . perish. . . . except you repent, you shall all . . . perish."

Suddenly I felt weak and was aware that my hands were trembling. "Repent? I must repent. But I don't know what that means. Tell me what that means."

"Let me show you, Victor."

Skillfully, the evangelist turned more pages. "Now read this, amigo."

Incredulity, then exhilaration, filled my mind as I read aloud, "Repent ye therefore, and be converted, that your sins may be blotted out, when the times of refreshing shall come from the presence of the Lord."

I put down the book. "Repent? Be converted? Sins blotted out?" It was all too great to comprehend. "Amigo, does this really mean that sins—*my sins*—can be blotted out?"

Eliecer nodded.

"What does that mean? Tell me, what does this all mean?"

"It means that even though you are a sinner—like all the rest of mankind, like myself—that your sins can be forgiven, blotted out, taken away, wiped out."

"It truly means all that?"

"Si, yes," Eliecer said softly. "That's what it means."

I pondered this silently for a while. Then, placing my finger in the Bible, I closed it and stood up. "Amigo, I must think about this for a while. It is too much for me to understand all at once."

Eliecer smiled. "I understand. I will come back."

"Soon?"

"Yes, soon."

"Gracias."

As Eliecer rode out of town on his burro, I returned to my seat on the bag of rice, my finger following the precious words, my lips moving as I read.

As yet there was not a single believer in my village. Nor was there one for miles around. I had nobody to turn to. I didn't know how to pray. I hardly knew how to read. But the Spirit of God was beginning to move in me, an unschooled farmer, even as He'd moved those other men I was reading about—the ones who had walked with Jesus.

Again and again I read all those Scriptures during those next days. I mulled over them, talked about them to my friends and customers, to my three women. I often neglected my work in order to read and to talk about what I was reading in the Word of God.

Villagers thought that I had actually become an Evangelical, though they apparently wondered why I still retained most of my old habits. Sometimes I would hear them talking.

"Victor must be an Evangelical, see how he reads from the Bible all the time?"

"And he talks about Jesus so much."

Nods all around.

"But," one spoke up. "He still smokes cigarettes and drinks rum. Do Evangelicals do that?"

Actually, what they said made little difference to me at that time. I was deeply concerned about the words Eliecer had shown me. And each day I read more and more that spoke to the deepest part of my life.

Those were wonderful yet difficult days for me. The more I read, the more I realized I must repent, must change my life. But I was not sure I was ready, or even willing, to do this. I enjoyed living the way I did. I didn't want to give it up. Yet I wanted the peace of God that Eliecer spoke so glowingly about.

Some nights I hardly slept at all.

But despite all that Eliecer told me, all I read, I comprehended so little. I had never heard of any of these things before. I was like a sponge, soaking it all up, but unable to absorb nourishment from all I took into myself.

Something had to happen soon. And it did.

I realized that even my family was laughing at me, sometimes to my face. But I cared little about that. The Word of God and Eliecer's love and compassion had left a deep mark upon me.

One day two teenage girls saw me reading the Bible. Giggling and silly, they approached. "Are you going to become an Evangelical?" they asked.

"I think I will," I replied, half in earnest, half teasing.

They looked at each other and laughed. One said, "Don't get mixed up with them. They swap wives!"

"Swap wives! The Evangelicals swap wives?"

"Yes, they do."

"*Caramba!*" I said. "Are you sure?"

They nodded, obviously delighted at the impact they'd made. I didn't know what to think. I needed to talk to Eliecer again. Two days later, the evangelist came back. As soon as I could, I went to see my friend. Eliecer was eating dinner when I arrived.

When he finished his meal, I said, "I've got a question for you."

"Okay, what is it?"

"I want the truth. Don't hedge."

"I'll answer the best I can."

"Is it true that Evangelicals swap wives?"

A slow grin spread across my friend's face. "Amigo, the answer is no! Somebody has told you something very untrue."

"Then it's not true? Not true at all?" I asked, feeling relieved, yet still doubtful.

Eliecer shook his head. He pointed to my Bible, which I now carried much of the time. "Read what Jesus says. He talks about sex, about women. And He tells us not to even desire our neighbor's wife."

His words started me thinking: wife, or wives? How stupid of me, I thought, to be concerned about "swapping wives" when I had three of them. Well, not really *wives*, but I was involved with all three. And, to some degree, I was supporting or helping support them all. What should I do?

With that thought came another. One of my women was a prostitute. Worse yet, I was engaged in the business of satisfying men's lusts. What would Jesus say about that?

3

I Want to Know the Way

The battle was really on now.

On the one hand, I could see the advantages of becoming an Evangelical: to possess the love, the kindness, the compassion I could see in Eliecer. I especially desired the peace he had. I was all too aware of these lacks in my own life: my own dark moods, the burden of my unforgiven sins, my frequent deep depressions, my inconsistencies.

But, on the other hand, I reasoned, to become one of "them," I'd have to give up too much.

How, I asked myself, *could I possibly give up my rum drinking and my three women? How could I choose just one of them to live with? How could I tell the others?* There seemed no way I could make the break or effect the change.

I didn't know at that time that I didn't have to do it. That Jesus Himself would do that.

Sometimes I almost wished I'd never seen that Bible! I loved it, feared it, revered it, held it in awe. "It even seems to know what I'm thinking!" I burst out one day, to nobody in particular. "It knows my heart—how wicked I am!"

And now, since my recent discussions with Eliecer, I

31

knew how the Bible defines that: It calls me a sinner. Though I hated to admit it, I knew the description was accurate. And, admitting that, I realized I must repent.

I had read where God had said that, clearly, precisely. So the battle raged.

Part of the time, I longed for Eliecer's return; part of the time, I dreaded his visits. But always, no matter how I felt, I would entertain him, sometimes hesitantly, reluctantly. Other times I'd be at my royal best, even playing for him my latest, hottest, loudest, honky-tonk jukebox records. This was so much a part of my life that it never occurred to me that Eliecer might not share my same enthusiasms and tastes in music.

There were days when my struggles were so intense that I wished my friend were there to talk with. Sometimes my defeat was so inglorious I wished Eliecer would never return, for how could I face him?

I knew by now that Eliecer's opening remark would be, "How are you doing on your Bible reading?"

And always, often against my will, when he'd ask the question, I'd admit the truth. Eliecer never rebuked me. He simply listened to my questions and my struggles. Then he'd open the Bible and share a new truth and pray for me. I had never prayed myself, and Eliecer was the first Evangelical I'd heard pray.

The few prayers I'd heard in the past had been ritualistic, powerless. But Eliecer's prayers were different. They were simple, specific, and powerful. It was obvious that the man wasn't merely saying words. He was actually talking to someone—to God?

This possibility alternately excited and frightened me. I wished I could know God as Eliecer apparently knew him. In my heart I knew such a relationship would be costly, too costly. So I hungered, and yet I resisted the fulfillment of that hunger.

A battle such as mine could not go on indefinitely. It had to find resolution. I knew that. Eliecer knew that. It must come to a head. But how? And when?

The showdown was different from anything we would have guessed.

It took place on the road from Buena Vista, the next village away, where I went to replenish my supply of rum. I started out that morning in a fairly jovial mood. Eliecer hadn't been to the village for several days. And since I had been avoiding reading the Bible for a while, life looked rather rosy.

Returning with my burro heavily laden with rum, God spoke to me through two women. "Buenos dias, Don Victor," one said.

"Buenos dias, señoras," I replied.

They took note of my cargo of liquor. "You still sell rum in your store?" It was more a statement than a question.

I nodded, suddenly apprehensive. "Si. . . ."

They looked at each other, then at me. "But, Don Victor, you're an Evangelical. . . ." Again it wasn't a question, it was a statement of fact. Lately I had begun to realize that most of the villagers considered me as such, because of my constant Bible reading and frequent visits from Eliecer.

Though I resisted the idea, I now knew I bore that label.

Not knowing how to answer, I said nothing and urged my burro to go on. But I wasn't quick enough to avoid the rest of their words.

". . . and Evangelicals don't buy rum, or use it, or even *sell* it."

Their words cut deeply into my heart, and I plodded on in misery. All at once, I resented Eliecer and his Evangelicals. I resented the position I found myself in. I groaned and asked myself, *Is it worth it? Is it really worth all this hassle?*

I'm always struggling. Eliecer's got something that gives him strength and power. I don't have it. I want it. Yet I don't. . . .

In my mind I heard a voice. It said, "Victor, you can't do it! You can't become an Evangelical! You can't give up everything: your business, your women, your rum. . . ."

I agreed. I didn't want to give it all up. I was tired of all this pressure. I was about to say, "To heck with it all!" because I was convinced I couldn't give up women and dancing and rum drinking in a hundred years.

Then I heard another voice. "Victor, what's a hundred years compared with eternity? Even if you could have twenty women. Even if you could have all the rum you could drink in a hundred years, it wouldn't be worth it!"

I was forced to agree with that voice, too.

Just then I remembered something I'd read about eternity. It told of a little bird that flew down to earth once every million years, picked up a grain of sand, and flew away. "By the time the earth is all gone," the tract had said, "eternity will have just begun!"

That illustration flashed through my mind.

It stopped me short. Just a few days before, I'd read about Jesus dividing the sheep from the goats. The goats would go to hell forever, it said. And the sheep would spend eternity with Him.

In that desperate moment, I saw God. He was looking down at me. His voice was full of power and judgment. I trembled as I heard Him say to me, "Victor, you didn't believe Me."

I saw all the people going past me. *They were going to hell!* And I heard God speak to me again. "Victor, you're going with them!"

I realized I was lost. I cried aloud, "There's no hope for me now. There's no chance to change!"

I could feel my soul. And it felt dirty, spotted. The thought pulsated in my mind, *How can I get my soul back, for just a little while, so I can repent?*

There on the trail that day, I truly thought all hope was gone.

The whole message of the Gospel came crashing upon me. And for the first time it was crystal clear: I was lost! I must repent! I must do it *now!*

I could resist no longer.

I nudged my burro off the trail into the grass and fell to my knees. "Before I die, I'll get right with You, God!" I cried. "I'll do whatever You want me to do, Lord. I don't care how much it costs. I've got to know You."

I had never prayed before. Not till that moment on the road. And never had I experienced such peace, such joy, such release as I felt now.

I tried to tell everybody about my joy.

And I couldn't understand when they wouldn't listen. Why wouldn't they respond?

What I didn't realize was that the entire village, the entire countryside in fact, was watching the transformation of Victor Landero. And they were numb with amazement! They could not comprehend such a complete turnabout.

Nor could I.

At first they actually couldn't believe what they were seeing: Victor Landero, the former turbulent, explosive, short-tempered bartender, was now the tranquil, peaceful evangelist. The changes had been dramatic, but there were more to come.

My life was so revolutionized that I was soon eagerly sharing my new experience with everybody who would listen, especially at my cantina.

Since I owned the place, I reasoned, and there's usually a crowd there, why not? I couldn't think of any good reasons why not. So I did. I shared my newfound faith joyfully, sometimes punctuating my remarks with generous swigs from my bottle of rum.

One day I was witnessing to a customer, pausing every few minutes to take a deep drag at my accustomed bottle, when he brought me up short. The man interrupted me right in the middle of a sentence.

"Victor," he said, "so you're an Evangelical?"

"Si, señor, I certainly am."

"Then what are you doing with that bottle of rum in your hand?"

I set the bottle down. "What's wrong with that?"

"Well, the Evangelicals I know, they don't drink."

I frowned, remembering the women's remarks on the trail. "They don't drink? Why not?"

"I'm not sure. I guess they figure it's not good for them or for their bodies."

I thought about that for a moment. Then I set the bottle aside. "If that's true, I won't drink either."

It wasn't long after that decision that Roberto Urda had invited me to drink with him, and I had refused. I can hardly blame him for getting upset and pouring the glass of beer on my head.

He was one of the first to accept this change in my life. He didn't want to; he was forced to. Shortly after the beer-pouring incident, Roberto came back.

"I have to talk to you, amigo," he said.

"I'm glad you came back," I told him. "I've wanted to talk to you."

"Victor," he began, scratching his head, "you are so—so different. I can't figure it all out."

He was nervous, but very much in earnest.

"I'm sorry I got so angry when you wouldn't drink with me. But it upset me. It really did. We've always had a few beers together. But what I really can't get straight is why you didn't get angry at me when I poured that beer on you."

I laughed. "I don't blame you for being so confused and

angry," I told him. "But, Roberto, it's a wonderful thing that's happened to me."

"Wonderful?" he asked cautiously. "You're an Evangelical now."

"Right. And let me tell you what that really means."

We talked for an hour that day. I told Roberto about finding the Bible in my suitcase, where I'd put it years before. I shared about reading it, about Eliecer, about my confusion, my struggles, my crisis on the road from Buena Vista.

Roberto shook his head. "I am impressed, amigo. And when I look at your life, I am—I am shamed. You are now so different from me. Even though we were the same for many years."

Roberto put his head in his hands, as though trying to comprehend all I had told him. When he looked up, there were tears in his eyes. "I can't get you out of my mind. After I poured beer on you and you didn't get mad, I thought and thought."

After a while, he arose. "I will be back, Victor. You must tell me more."

"Of course," I said. "Maybe I will read to you from my Bible. Maybe that will help you to understand."

One evening Roberto did return. He was already half-drunk when he slumped in a chair in my cantina and ordered a beer. When I served him, he grabbed my hand. "Victor, amigo. Wait."

"Sure, Roberto. What do you want?"

"When you read the book—the Bible—it changed your life?"

"Yes, amigo. It changed my life."

"You said you would read that book to me. Will you do it now?"

"I will be glad to." I got my Bible that was already getting worn and ragged. Since I had never attended school, my reading was slow, laborious. Like a child, I had to follow the lines with my finger and sound out each word.

Roberto didn't mind. This was all new to him, and he needed the time to hear each word. But, even as interested as he was, his drink-soaked mind soon got drowsy, and his head began to nod. I kept on reading. Here was the chance I'd been waiting for, and I was going to make the most of it.

Roberto's head fell forward on his chest. He jerked it up and tried to open his eyes. Then he gave up and slumped over on the table and began to snore.

I shook him. "Wake up, Roberto! Wake up!"

No response.

Then came the idea: Pray for Roberto to wake up. "Lord, wake him up. Take away his sleep!"

Instantly Roberto sat up. His eyes popped wide open. He was wide awake, with no sign of sleepiness. And, miraculously, he was stone sober. He blinked at me in amazement. "I heard you pray for God to wake me up."

I was as surprised as Roberto.

"Such power!" Roberto exclaimed. "I've never seen God answer a prayer like that! In the big church there is much praying, but no power. Nothing happens. But you pray just a few words, and I wake up. I'm wide awake. I'm sober! It is a miracle!"

This time, when Roberto left the cantina, he was a changed man.

I continued to read my Bible. I carried it with me practically everywhere I went. And every day I told someone the wonderful things God had done for me. Inevitably, I met with opposition.

Since my cantina was so close to the road, and I was such a notably new Evangelical, I became the target of many cultists. They would stop by and debate with me, trying to prove that I had made a wrong decision.

Many times they left me in confusion. When Eliecer came, we talked about the problem. "They all tell me, 'Our way is the right way. Our way is the truth. Yours is wrong.' Don Eliecer, what shall I do?"

"You must turn to the Word of God," Eliecer finally answered. "You must allow God to give you the answers from His Word. If you soak yourself in His Word, He will do just what you ask. He will give you the right answers to their questions—and to yours."

I knew this was the answer. "I'll do it," I told him. "I will learn to know God better than I know myself. I will study very hard."

"And I will be praying for you."

From that time on I spent more time studying the Scriptures than ever before, trusting God to help me. The answer wasn't long in coming. One day I read the words Jesus spoke to His disciples during a time when they were confused. Jesus told them: "I am the way, the truth, and the life. . . ."

That was what I had been looking for. "That's my answer!

Jesus is the way. He is the truth. He is the life. He is my answer!"

In my excitement I walked around the room, praising God.

"If Christ is the way," I told Eliecer when I saw him again, "I want to know the way, so I'll follow Christ only. If He is the truth and I want to know the truth that sets men free, then I'll get the truth from Him. And if Christ is the life, and I want life, I'll get that life from Him. I will follow only Christ!"

I was in dead earnest about my desire to follow Jesus, wherever and however, and I began to fully trust the Spirit of God to guide me into all truth.

I was immediately faced with a difficult decision: what about the prostitutes? Was it right for an Evangelical to be living off the proceeds of a brothel?

I decided the answer was no. So I dismissed the prostitutes, closed the bar and dance hall, and converted the establishment into a general store.

Soon I was faced with something else: the proper use of the Lord's Day. As I studied the New Testament, I learned that the early Christians dedicated Sunday to the Lord. Up till this time, I had never done that. I usually spent Sunday in my store, which soon became a shopping center for the surrounding area.

How can I close on Sunday? I wondered. It was my biggest day for business. Farmers came to town on Saturday with all their produce to sell in the markets. On Sunday they'd stock up for the coming week from my store. How could I afford to close that day?

Monday was my slowest day of the week for business. If I closed my store on Sunday, it might seriously endanger my business. But if I kept it open on the Lord's Day, it would be at the expense of my spiritual growth.

What should I do?

For a while I carried on a running argument with the Lord, who seemed clearly to indicate closing the store on Sunday.

Finally I decided to see if I could strike a bargain with Him. "I'll tell You what," I said. "I'll close the store for one Sunday. And if I don't lose money, I might try it again. Otherwise, don't ask me to do it again."

So with fear and trembling, I closed the store that next Sunday, despite the warnings of friends: "It'll ruin you!"

Monday morning I opened, expecting the worst. But, to my surprise, I sold twice as much that day as I had ever sold on any day before! From that time on I never questioned the Lord, even when it didn't seem logical to me.

But now I was faced with what was probably the most difficult decision of my life. I was living with three women. As an Evangelical I knew I should have only one wife.

Which one should I keep? How could I decide?

At best it would be a difficult decision. I had lived with all of them: one who worked in my brothel as a prostitute, one who lived in a nearby village, one who lived on my farm with me. I agonized over the decision for a long time.

Finally, after lots of prayer, I decided on Teresa, the third one, *if she would come to Christ*.

I told her about it. Then I waited.

Teresa realized at once that she had the advantage over

me. I had been a difficult man to live with. I had often humiliated her and had always kept her in subjection. She had never known for sure when I'd be coming home. And even though our culture accepts that kind of life-style, Teresa had been deeply resentful that I regularly shared my love with others.

Now was her chance for revenge. And she took it.

Previously Teresa had been mild and gentle, but when I took my foot off her, she became rebellious and impertinent. For quite a while I wondered if I'd made the right choice.

For instance, when I would ask her to prepare my breakfast, she would laugh. "Why should I?" she said. "Get your own!"

Other times she would become sarcastic. "You've always got a piece of paper in your hand (my Bible, a tract, or a newspaper), why don't you eat that! If you're so hungry, eat paper. That'll fill you up!"

I became so disturbed by Teresa's attitude that I took the matter to Eliecer and the new friends I had made at the Bible institute where he had studied and asked them to pray for me. After a while, the situation improved. God answered their prayers. About six months later, Teresa, of her own free will, decided to come to Christ. Since then she has been loving and obedient, a good mother to our children.

Still, she was not legally my wife. And I longed for the day when we could cut through the governmental red tape and become man and wife.

4

Costly Decisions

My family couldn't help but notice the incredible change that came over my life. One by one they, too, accepted Jesus. Gregorio, my younger brother, was one of the first. He was fiery, aggressive, charming, full of initiative. We had learned long ago to treat him with care. When he got upset or angry, he would simply walk out of the house and leave us.

Once he was gone for three years.

Gregorio was talented, with good financial instincts, and he frankly loved to make money. He bought his first accordion at the age of ten and was soon making good money playing for fiestas and baptisms.

"Even baptisms turn into fiestas," Gregorio told me. "And I don't really care which of the two I play for. They both pay me well."

With the money he saved, he bought our family's farm and home and thus became his own family's landlord.

Shortly after I became a Christian, I showed my Bible to Gregorio and tried to tell him what God was doing in my life.

"None of it makes any sense to me," he said. "I don't feel like a sinner. . . ."

After a while I just left him alone.

Gregorio loved me, though, and was pleased with the change in my life. He simply felt that "all of that evangelical stuff" was not for him.

Gregorio did go to the evangelical meetings, partly out of curiosity and partly because there was nothing else to do on Sunday. In our area, radio and TV were still practically unknown, so any social gathering was usually attended by everybody.

Gregorio heard the Scriptures read so many times that he memorized many of them. He didn't consciously commit them to memory; it just happened.

The same thing is often the case in my area of Colombia. I know of some pastors who even now can neither read nor write and must have someone else read the Scriptures for them. They listen so intently that they memorize large portions of Scripture.

It was so with Gregorio. The Word of God filled his uncluttered mind. And at an opportune time the Holy Spirit used that stored Word to bring him to Himself.

It happened to Gregorio at a dance.

He was thoroughly enjoying himself, playing his accordion. "It's a mighty curious thing to me," Gregorio told me later, "that God should attend a dance. But He certainly did that night—the night He found me."

Somebody had given Gregorio a small New Testament that he began carrying around with him. "I don't really

know why I did it," he said. "I just did. I even took it with
me to the dance that particular night, in my hip pocket."

By three o'clock in the morning, the dance was in full
swing. Many of the dancers were drunk, and the party was
noisy and boisterous. Gregorio began playing an especially
romantic song, one that he liked very much.

"I was giving it everything I had," he told me, "when
something strange happened. I became very deeply moved
and began to cry. At first I didn't realize it was God moving
in my life, and I tried to continue. But I couldn't!"

He stopped playing. And the dancing stopped.

Suddenly Gregorio was the center of attention. "What's
happening, amigo?" someone asked.

My brother didn't answer. He had his head down in his
arms and the tears were flowing down his cheeks. "I was
embarrassed," he said. "But for some reason there was an
even greater concern; one I couldn't even define."

Someone said, "He's a little drunk."

"No, Gregorio doesn't drink that much."

"What's the matter then?"

"I think he's having a love affair with some pretty
señorita, and this romantic song just got to him."

After a few minutes, Gregorio picked up his accordion
and tried again to play. Again he had to stop.

"People came to me and begged me to go on," Gregorio
said. "They thought I was playing hard to get, and they
offered me more money to keep on playing. Some people
got angry and shouted at me. It made no difference. I just
couldn't keep on going."

Gregorio told me how words from the Bible came flooding through his mind. "I heard Jesus saying, 'Peace I leave with you, my peace I give unto you. . . . Peace I leave with you. . . .'

"Over and over again I heard those words. But I didn't have peace. I felt miserable. And yet Jesus kept saying, 'Peace I give unto you. . . . Peace. . . . Peace. . . .'"

Gregorio said that the more he heard the words, the more moved he became. He looked across the dance hall and was appalled. "I had never seen it quite like that before. At that time, the party was in a sad state. I saw drunkenness, and I was disgusted. Jesus was talking to me about the peace I didn't see and didn't possess. I couldn't go on any longer. I closed my accordion and put my head in my arms and cried."

The whole crowd in the cantina begged him to continue. Finally Gregorio asked a friend to take over, and he went to his room, which was in the same building. Weeping almost uncontrollably, Gregorio threw himself across his bed.

He told me, "I could hear Jesus talking about peace. But I didn't have any peace. All I could think of was that I had been used by the devil—my playing made people jump around and act silly and get drunk.

"I saw the picture clearly for the first time, and it wasn't very pretty. And all the time I wept and wept."

People came and begged him to come back to the dance. He forced them out of his room and began to pray. "Words poured out of me. I told God I was sorry and that if He would use me I would do anything."

I came to the Lord early in 1956. Gregorio's conversion was just eight months later. True to his word, Gregorio obeyed God's leading and went to Bible school for a couple of years. He is a natural leader and an excellent evangelist. Eventually he was receiving invitations to come and preach all over northern Colombia.

With his business mind, had he chosen to do so, I believe my brother could have become wealthy. Instead, he chose to follow Jesus Christ. It was a costly decision: after a while all his money and his farm were gone.

Meanwhile, I was having problems of my own.

From the very first, I shared my new life with everybody I met. I wanted to. I loved to. But it was more than a mere desire. It was an irresistible compulsion.

It seemed that nothing else mattered.

I remember once having to go for six days without telling anyone about Jesus. I thought I would burst. Everywhere I went I just *had* to share my good news. I talked about Jesus in the cantina until I closed it and made it into a store, and then I talked to my store customers about Jesus. I talked to them while I was weighing sugar for them or while I loaded a sack of rice on man's burro. Sometimes my voice was hoarse at night from talking about Jesus all day long.

When people came to me, I told them about Jesus. But there were those who didn't come to me, people who lived in the jungle or in distant villages. I began going out and telling them, too. Sometimes I'd leave my store for days at a time.

At first it didn't matter. Things seemed to go well while I was gone. But, inevitably, things began to change. I began to notice that sometimes the money didn't balance; the stock had dwindled too low; the place was in disorder; there was too much credit on the books, and so on. Once when I returned from an evangelization journey, the situation was very bad. So I made a decision.

I told my wife, "I'm not going out anymore."

I didn't sleep very well that night.

And the next morning, when I went out on my patio to pray, God directed me to some words that changed everything. First Corinthians 15:58 says: "Therefore, my beloved brethren, be ye stedfast, unmoveable, always abounding in the work of the Lord, forasmuch as ye know that your labour is not in vain in the Lord."

"God," I prayed, "I'm sorry. I forgot for a little while. I will keep going out to tell others." I told Him that day, and I meant it, that I would keep on telling others of His love, no matter what it cost.

Eventually, it cost me everything.

I had always allowed credit, and I'd usually been able to collect. Now I noticed that for some reason the accounts were getting larger. And the collections were more difficult. I soon learned the reason.

"Why?" one of my best customers asked. "You ask why they won't pay you now?"

"Yes," I said. "It bothers me. I want to be fair, but sometimes it becomes difficult."

He shrugged. "The reason, my brother, is that you're

now an Evangelical. They know you won't force them to pay. So they keep on getting credit. And they'll keep on till they ruin you!"

The man was right on both counts. I steadfastly refused to demand payment. God had been good to me. I wanted to show mercy to others. The foreseeable result was financial ruin, which wasn't long in coming.

Finally things got so bad I closed my store. From a man of considerable means, I was now reduced to nothing. My passion to tell others about Jesus had cost me everything I owned, even my livelihood.

I told my wife, "I can't complain. Jesus has given me new life. His hand is guiding me. He will take care of me."

So I bought a horse and loaded it with cookware, medicines, a few staple goods, and Bibles. I began traveling around to homes and villages, selling my wares.

I did sell my goods. But mostly I gave away my most cherished possession: the knowledge that Jesus Christ had come into the world to transform a man's life. This I did with great abandon and success.

Shortly after my store went broke and I sold it, I moved to the tiny village of Corozalito and bought a farm from Calixto Amante. It was there we began seeing God perform miracles that eventually attracted the attention of thousands of Colombians. Within a short time, there was scarcely an individual, or a family, or a village in the San Jorge River basin, who had not been introduced to the life-changing message of Jesus.

I had no idea how much of an impact this was having on

others, including the organization which was to become a vital part of my life: the Latin America Mission. They first heard about what was happening among us early in 1958, when missionary Bob Reed visited the area.

He returned to Cartagena with a report they had difficulty believing: "It's almost impossible to even get there!" he told Field Director David Howard and the others. "I had to go by burro, dugout canoe, and on foot. But everywhere I went I came across whole settlements of believers! Hundreds of them!

"I asked them who the missionaries were, and when they had come. They told me there had never been any missionaries there. I asked them how all this had happened. Every time they shook their heads and mentioned a name I had never heard of—Victor Landero.

"The man's incredible!" Bob Reed told them. "Simply incredible!"

They called me incredible. But I knew they were wrong. There's nothing incredible about me at all. Only God's power can change lives. Knowing what I did of God's love and of Jesus' command for His followers to keep on telling others, I couldn't stop telling others about Him.

God did the rest.

David Howard heard so much about what was happening in our area (they called it *spontaneous combustion*) that he decided to visit us. Several times we heard he was coming, but he never made it. Satan seemed to hinder every effort he made to reach us. It wasn't until two years later that he came to Corozalito, and we were able to meet.

In those days, Corozalito consisted of only four bamboo-sided thatched huts. Today the village boasts three streets and perhaps thirty such huts. It was situated in the heart of the jungle, in a tiny clearing, three hard days' journey from the coastal city of Cartagena.

For an outsider to visit Corozalito, it required an interminable bus ride, then several hours in a jeep to the end of the trail. From there it was still nearly a full day's ride upriver in a *Jonson* (a Johnson Sea Horse-powered dugout canoe), then a three-hour hike.

Today you can make the entire trip in a comfortable, twenty-minute flight in one of MAFs (Missionary Aviation Fellowship) Cessna 180s.

In Corozalito I felt God was directing me to continue my ministry. Calixto Amante, from whom I purchased my small farm, had had a passing contact with the Gospel. He owned a large tract of land, which included the village of Corozalito.

Corozalito was the unknown jungle clearing where the Holy Spirit was to visit with such force and power. Why God chose this unmapped village as the setting for this time of great blessing can only be explained as one of His unexplainable sovereign acts.

But sovereign act it was—as is confirmed by the scores of congregations, and hundreds—even thousands—of believers who are today scattered across Colombia.

In Corozalito, I began discipling Calixto. I spent a lot of time with him, sharing the Word and discussing the principles of living for Jesus. Working together, it wasn't long before a strong core of believers was formed, a church built, and a center for evangelism developed.

Calixto, though his nature was to remain quietly in the background, was soon deeply involved in the ministry. He became one of the primary leaders in the church.

No more than one hundred people ever lived in Corozalito, though its "community" included many outlying farms. Our first small bamboo chapel has long since been outgrown and replaced, and the present one is constructed of cement blocks.

Our vigorous evangelism paid off. And when David Howard visited us two years later, I was happy to report, "Of the ninety-four people living in and near Corozalito, ninety-two are believers."

I took David to visit one of the remaining nonbelievers. When this twenty-year-old woman invited us in, I began sharing Christ with her. As before, she was noncommittal and reserved.

Finally, in exasperation, I said, "Why in the world don't you accept the Lord? You know everybody else here is Christian. You know the truth. You know what you ought to do. How come you don't do it?"

The girl shrugged and dug a bare toe in the dirt. She refused to open her heart to the Gospel.

I was upset when we left, and I asked David Howard, "How can she hold out? In a village like this, where everybody is Christian except two, how can she resist?"

David opened his Bible and read from 2 Corinthians 4:4 about how "the god of this world" has blinded those who

don't believe, "lest the light of the glorious gospel of Christ
. . . should shine unto them."

That made sense to me. Suddenly the picture became
clear.

"It must be like something that happens in the woods," I
said. "Everybody out here has his own dugout canoe.
When a sudden flood comes, the water rises very quickly."

David agreed, "Yes, sometimes five to ten feet in no time
at all."

"Right. And when that happens, the canoes that are tied
up by the riverbank will get ripped loose and be swept down
the river."

I could see David didn't know for sure what I was talking
about, so I explained. "If you see a flood coming and the
river is rising and canoes are being swept away, well, if you
see that your canoe is still there, you're going to run to the
river and tie it up as tight as you can, so it won't get swept
away. Right?"

"Right," David said, still not quite sure of my point.

"That's what's happening to the devil's canoes," I explained. "There's a great rising of the Holy Spirit. The devil
sees one canoe after the other being swept down the river.
He's only got two of them left.

"He runs and ties them up tight, so they can't break
loose."

"That's exactly right," David agreed. "That's why the two
are able to resist. The devil has got them tied up tightly to
the bank."

As soon as I got my farm in order and my crops planted, I

began going out to evangelize again. It was in my blood. As I said before, I felt I had to tell others. I often wished I didn't have to work on the farm, so I could spend all my time telling people about Jesus.

One day I remembered the bargain I'd made with the Lord about closing my store on Sunday. He had honored our deal and had given me more business on Monday than I would have had on Sunday. I decided to try another bargain.

I said to God, "One day of the week already belongs to You. But I'd be willing to make a fifty-fifty arrangement for the other six days. So, if You'll help me keep my farm in order and my family cared for by my working only three days a week, then I'll give the other three days to You.

"And, God, during the extra days You give me, I'll go out and tell people about how much You love them."

The Lord seemed agreeable, so I began taking four full days each week to spread the news of this better life. God did such a good job with His part that I found I could soon begin keeping my farm going by working on it only two days a week.

Before long, I was spending five days each week doing the Lord's work. After all, He promised He would bless those who honor Him. I just took Him at His Word.

When I first began talking to people about Jesus, I didn't quite know how to reach them. Most of them knew very little about God, and nothing about His Son. I remembered how God gave Moses the words to speak when he went to Pharaoh. So I asked Him to do the same for me.

Finally, I developed a dialogue that worked, even with
the most backward and untaught. An example of this was
my conversation with Luis. After we had talked about his
health, his family, his crops, and the like, I asked, "Do you
know who Jesus Christ is?"

"No," he said.

"Do you know what the Bible is?"

"No."

"Do you know what sin is?"

"No."

"Have you ever heard of Adam and Eve?"

"No."

"Do you know anything about God?"

"No."

Having established all this, I said, "God is the One who
made the world. He put two people in the world: Adam and
Eve. He told them they could have anything they wanted,
except the fruit from one tree. And what do you suppose
they did?"

"I don't know. Eat that fruit?"

"Yes. Adam and Eve took the one thing God had told
them not to touch! That was disobeying God. That's called
sin. So God had to punish them. Every man who has lived
since then has sinned against God.

"But God still loved the people He had made. He wanted
to do something for them. He had one Son up in heaven.
He decided to send that Son to earth to help the men He
had made."

As I spoke to Luis, the Holy Spirit made him responsive.

Then I opened my New Testament.

"For God so loved the world, that He gave His only be-gotten Son. . . ."

Almost every time I presented such a loving Father, who so sacrificially gave His Son, the listeners would open their hearts and receive Him.

Not till the missionaries came and showed such surprise at the almost universal acceptance of my simple presentation, did I realize it could possibly be otherwise.

5

The Power of the Spirit

The church at Corozalito grew so well and so fast that I soon noticed a spirit creeping in that troubled me. It was difficult to define, but it was, well, it was as if the church wasn't as healthy as it had been.

I talked to Calixto and Gregorio about it. "I feel uneasy," I said, "as though we're beginning to slip into some sort of rut."

Calixto agreed. "Instead of looking to Jesus, it's more like looking to ourselves."

Even though the Lord had blessed me many times, I had to admit I didn't always trust Him. "I've been going out so much lately," I said, "that my farm is suffering. I feel the financial strain. I need to trust Jesus more for my needs."

We discussed some of the other needs and problems of the group. We prayed about them. We prayed for a long time. And when we finished, I said, "I'm going to begin a study in the Book of Acts. I believe we've got to pattern ourselves more after the early Church than we are doing."

The more I read the Book of Acts, the more I felt God wanted to visit us with a mighty outpouring of His Holy Spirit. I did begin sharing the Book of Acts with the church. It was hard work for me, because I had to stay ahead of them. But the farther we went, the more excited I felt.

"This is good!" I told Gregorio. "This is what we need."

I didn't think about it at the time, but the stage was being set for God to pour Himself out upon the church. My entire family had come to the Lord. I was now free from my business entanglements. And I was situated in the very heart of an unevangelized area.

Along with Calixto Amante, my brothers Gregorio and Claudio, and a few others, I was going out regularly to visit and preach. But there seemed to be something lacking. We needed more love, more compassion, and more power.

I began to pray that God would give it to us.

One day I decided to spend time alone with the Lord and set out walking. I hardly noticed where I was going. And, after a while, I found myself on a ridge overlooking the valley. I stood there for a long time, praying and meditating.

Suddenly I felt uneasy, as though I was being watched. It was as if an evil presence of some kind was there. It was so strange, so unfamiliar, that I was frightened.

I looked all around, but saw nothing unusual. I looked behind me, behind trees, everywhere. Though I saw no person or animal, I still felt that presence. I was accustomed to the presence of God. But this was something different. I surmised that I had stumbled into an area where witchcraft was being practiced. Feeling uneasy, I quickly left.

Everywhere I went, I was surrounded by thick jungle. Finally I came to a tiny clearing on the hillside. And there, at the foot of a huge tree, I fell on my knees and poured out my heart to God.

"O God, give us more power," I prayed. "Fill us to overflowing with Your Spirit. Give us more love for one another."

I don't know how long I was there, but after a while God's healing presence came and eased the heavy weight of my load. I went home greatly refreshed.

The place now had special meaning for me, and I returned often to pray and fast. I shared the spot with Calixto, Gregorio, and others who also came with me on occasion.

Before long, most of the congregation came here for special times of worship, and we called the little clearing Mizpah, after the place where the Hebrews were victorious over the Philistines.

We cleared the area and were soon using the spot regularly.

We spent more and more time in prayer and heart searching. And it all began bearing fruit in a most unusual manner.

Juan Gonzalez was a young man, about eighteen years of age. He had come from a very poor family. He told me on several occasions, "Victor, I don't think I will ever amount to anything."

"God can change that," I told him.

"I don't know," he said. "I have feelings of great unworthiness at times. My body has been sick so often. . . ."

After coming to the Lord in 1959, Juan's attitude

changed somewhat. But he still had deep feelings of inferiority and inadequacy and was often deeply depressed.

One night I was away from the church at Corozalito when something very unusual took place—something that powerfully changed Juan's life—and mine.

Juan told me about it when I returned.

"It was during my prayer time," he said. "I was praying aloud as is my custom, but not loudly or in a disorderly fashion. I was praying quietly. You know how I pray."

I nodded. Juan was one of the quietest persons I knew. He never did anything out of the way or different that might attract attention to him.

"I was kneeling," Juan continued. "I had been praying for a long time when it happened."

"When what happened?" I asked.

"Well, I don't know exactly what happened. Anyway, I was praying as I usually do, when suddenly I didn't recognize the words I was saying."

"Didn't recognize them?"

"No," Juan said firmly. "I seemed to be praying in a different language, one foreign to me. Though it was unfamiliar to me, it had a pleasing sound. I rather liked what I heard myself praying. . . ."

Something began to register in my mind. Something from the Book of Acts. Could it be that God was sending Pentecost to Corozalito?

"Had you ever prayed like this before?"

Juan shook his head. I was noticing something different about him today. A new assurance, a sort of glow, something I couldn't quite put my finger on.

I leaned back in my chair. Excitement was growing in me. Before I spoke again, Juan said, "I felt as if I was praising God in a new language, a different tongue, so to speak. . . ."

"Different tongue, you said?"

"Yes, Victor, that's what it seemed to be. It was not as if it was my tongue at all. Anyway, it was refreshing, pleasant."

Juan got a serious look on his face. "Victor, what's this all about? What's happening to me?"

I shook my head. "I don't know for sure. Before I answer, I want to ask you a couple of questions."

"Sure. Anything."

"Do you sense anything different in yourself now? I mean since that experience. More freedom? More love? More power?"

He nodded. "Yes, I do. I have all of those. But there's something else. You know how sick I've been for so long?"

"Yes."

"Well, Victor, I think God is healing me. I feel free. I feel as if I am special to God. As if He loves me in a new way. I feel clean and washed."

"Like being baptized?" I asked. "Immersed in the Holy Spirit?"

His face lit up. "Yes. That's it. Yes! That's exactly what it feels like. I've been baptized—inside and out!"

I opened my Bible and read from the Book of Acts. As I read, I knew that this was what we had been praying for: the power, the effectiveness, the healing, the inward cleansing. This must be what Jesus meant when He told the disciples to wait till they received the power from on high.

"Juan," I said slowly, "I believe you've received the filling of the Holy Spirit."

Juan looked pleased, then puzzled. "But why *me?* Why did it happen to me? Why didn't it happen to you?"

That question puzzled me. Why hadn't it happened to me? When Juan left, I talked to God about it. "Lord, I thank You for filling my brother with Your presence, Your power, Your Holy Spirit. Is this, then, the beginning? Are You going to pour out Your Holy Spirit upon the rest of the church?"

As I prayed, I felt an expectancy that I hadn't noticed before. I believed God was going to come to me in a special way.

I had never heard of anybody speaking in tongues—though at the time I didn't know what to call the phenomenon—and I was excited about Juan's new experience. So were Calixto and Gregorio. In fact, I think we were more excited about it than he was. Juan didn't really talk about it very much. But he moved with a new assurance. Anyone could tell something significant had happened to him.

Some of the brothers told him, "You are like Timothy now. And now that you have the power of the Holy Spirit, you should go out and preach."

That seemed reasonable to the rest of us. Because wasn't that why the Holy Spirit was promised? When we talked to Juan about preaching, though, he didn't agree. "I don't think I am called to preach," he said.

"But the Holy Spirit has come upon you as it happened in the Book of Acts," I said.

"Maybe the Holy Spirit gives some the power to preach," Juan said, "but I believe He has come to me for a different purpose, not preaching."

"For what purpose?" I asked.

"For healing from my mental and physical problems, to make me less timid, to free me from my past. . . ."

He might be right, I thought, knowing a little bit of his struggles. As an orphan, Juan had suffered all kinds of feelings of failure and inadequacy. Perhaps the Holy Spirit was healing him, empowering him to overcome in different ways.

Some of the others didn't agree.

They kept telling Juan, "You should be able to preach now."

"Try it. . . . You'll do a wonderful job."

Finally, I decided we should give Juan a chance to find out for himself. I asked him to go along with me. When it came time for the message, I told the people that Juan was going to preach. Most of them had heard about Juan's experience, so they were eager to hear him.

But Juan just couldn't do it. He got up in front of the people and tried to speak. He tried. He really tried. But it seemed the words just wouldn't come out. I felt sorry for him. Several times afterwards, when he went with me, I would ask him to come up front.

"I'll speak first, then you say a few words," I told him.

"I'll try."

That didn't work either. He just wasn't cut out for preaching, even though he had been filled with the Holy Spirit. Despite his seeming failure in that area, Juan did begin to blossom in other ways.

I was impressed by his new stability, his new power in prayer, his daily, consistent walk with the Lord. When I talked to him about these things, he agreed.

"For the first time in my life, I feel free," he said. "I feel as though God is opening up my mind in new ways. I believe He has given me a new heart and spirit, as He said He would. Now I can see and think as I've never been able to do. I praise Him for it all!"

Juan's life has since borne out all he told me that day.

Meanwhile, I was spending more time with the Lord than I had ever done. Along with all the believers in Corozalito, I redoubled my intensive study of the Book of Acts.

Two weeks after Juan's experience, I was leading in a prayer at the church, when I was suddenly aware that I was praying in a language unknown to me. As with Juan, I was conscious that I was speaking to God, even praising Him, though I had no comprehension of the words I was saying.

It was a beautiful experience. I felt aglow with a new sense of God's love and had a new awareness of Jesus' life in me. For days I was full of praise and worship, and gratitude to God seemed to well up within me continuously.

"What do you think this will mean to our group?" Calixto asked me. "How do you feel about it?"

"I'm encouraged," I told him. "I believe what is happening is a confirmation of what we're reading in the Book of Acts—that it's for us today—now. It makes me believe that God wants to bless all of us—at Corozalito and everywhere. That's what Peter said on the Day of Pentecost."

Though I truly believed what I had just said, I didn't know exactly what to do about my experience. I felt that every believer should be filled with the Holy Spirit.

But I did not then, nor do I now believe that the evidence of this infilling is necessarily speaking in an unknown tongue or language. After discussing the matter at length with some of the believers, I decided we should go and talk to Claudio.

Claudio, my baby brother, had come to the Lord several months after I had and was now pastoring in a nearby village. I wasn't sure how he would receive the news of the happenings at Corozalito, but I felt we must tell him.

As a young man, Claudio had been much like me. We both enjoyed fiestas, drinking rum and beer. We both loved the ladies. But, for some reason, Claudio didn't like dancing. He said, "Dancers are *poco loco*, a little crazy!" Maybe he is right.

He was into witchcraft in those days and was very good at casting spells on people to gain control over them. He liked Eliecer, as I did, and would always come to hear him preach. I'll never forget the night Claudio came to Christ. I had invited Eliecer to my house to preach, and, when it came time, the house was full. My brother was up front where he could watch and hear Eliecer.

Eliecer was telling about the time Jesus said, "Come to

me, all you who labour and are heavy laden, and I will give you rest."

When Eliecer finished and asked, "Who would like to follow Jesus?" Claudio stood up and turned his life over to the Master.

Despite his former life, Claudio's walk with the Lord seemed to come easily to him. I remember how I envied him, because he hadn't seemed to struggle with so many different problems, as I had done.

Before long, Claudio would go out with me when I preached and soon developed into a good preacher. He was sensitive to the leadings of the Holy Spirit, had a fine sense of humor, and knew how to talk to people. After a couple of years, he began pastoring a small church.

Claudio and I seldom had any disagreements. Now as we approached his farm, I wondered if today's discussion might result in one. He was working when we got there, but stopped and greeted us.

"Come into my house," he said. "We will have something to cool our throats."

As we drank lemonade, we had our customary palaver—discussing several things before we approached our subject—the Colombian way. It is considered poor taste to get immediately into the purpose of your visit. After we had talked for a while, I decided it was time.

"You are very zealous for the Lord, my brother," I said.

He nodded. "Yes. I want Jesus to have the best of my life."

"Have you been going out evangelizing much lately?" Gregorio asked.

"Yes. Some of us have gone many days' walk from here. We have shared the Gospel with many new people."

"And many have been coming to Jesus?"

He nodded, beaming. "Yes. God is so very good!"

Finally, I said, "We have a special purpose in coming. . . ."

"I thought so."

"The Holy Spirit has fallen upon the church at Corozalito," I said, "something similar to the Book of Acts."

His face clouded. "Similar to the Book of Acts?" he asked cautiously.

"Yes, first it was Juan, then, a couple of weeks later, I myself received the filling of the Holy Spirit."

He began to squirm. "How do you know the Holy Spirit anointed you?" he asked. "How did He tell you He had done this?"

"Because we spoke in tongues. . . ." I began.

"Spoke in tongues!" he exploded. "That is wrong! It is not correct! One of the missionaries told me. That is from the demons, not from God. You have been deceived."

I shook my head. "My brother, please listen to me. . . ."

For the next few minutes I told him the story: about how neither Juan nor I had been seeking this phenomenon. It had been a spontaneous act from God Himself. I told him I now felt more in tune with God, more at peace with my fellow believers, and I had had more power in ministry.

"What about Juan?" he asked. "Did it make him into a preacher?" He also knew how shy and backward Juan had been, so filled with feelings of personal failure and shortcomings, and how he had been ill most of the time for a number of years.

"No," I said. "It didn't make him into a preacher."

"Then what good is it?"

"Juan is a transformed man," I told him. "He has experienced much healing, both in his body and in his mind. He praises God now, all the time. And you know he seldom did that before."

"That's right," Claudio said slowly. Then he shook his head vigorously. "No, Victor. I do not wish to become involved. Even if this anointing does what you say, I don't want any part in it."

"That is your choice," I told him. "I felt it was my duty to tell you all that God is doing in my life. This experience is so new, so powerful, so wonderful. I am filled with joy myself all the time. I thought you would like to hear. . . ."

He nodded. "Yes, Victor, I do thank you for coming. But I have a good relationship with the missionaries, and I fear this—this speaking in tongues—might change that. No, my brother, I do not wish to become involved in this new thing with you."

I didn't wish to anger him. Nor did I wish to leave him till he had heard me out. "It has been good, brother—very good. It has caused a great serenity among all the people who gather at Corozalito—a serenity and peace. We feel like new persons. We are in harmony together."

"All right, Victor," he said. "I believe you. I believe it has happened to you. I admit I am prejudiced. But I am very careful. I ask you to be careful, too."

"My brother," I said, "I know this comes from God."

"If it comes from God, I will accept it," he said. "If it is the truth, then I want it."

The time had come, I knew. "We have come to tell you what has happened and to pray with you."

He agreed. "Okay. Let's pray."

So we entered into a time of prayer. I prayed silently, as did the others. For some reason, we didn't feel like praying aloud. Claudio's wife was there, kneeling beside her husband. I could hear her whisper to Claudio, "Be careful—be very careful."

Claudio wasn't saying anything. I don't even know if he was praying, because I didn't hear him utter a word. We prayed a long time, hours, I think. Suddenly, I wanted to lay my hands on my brother, so I got up and went to him.

I touched him on the shoulder very lightly and prayed quietly. I felt Claudio tremble a little. I moved my hand to the top of his head. That was when I felt the power of God come.

Claudio began trembling almost uncontrollably. He burst out praying. And the words that came were not his own. He was praising God in a language that was strange to me, one I had never heard before.

While Claudio prayed, I sensed a light in the room, though I didn't see it, because I didn't open my eyes. It didn't seem proper to open them. This was a holy moment; Jesus was in the room.

Claudio knelt upright, raised his hands, spreading his arms wide. A torrent of words flowed from his lips. On and on it went, a veritable flood of living water from his innermost being.

A long time later, Claudio jumped up and embraced me
and the others. "So this is the fullness of the Holy Spirit!" It
was not a question. "This is the fullness. . . ." He began
laughing and crying, both at once.

Then he sat down. "I must think about this," he said. "It
is so wonderful—wonderful."

He looked astonished, excited, pensive, much as I had
felt just a few days before when this had happened to me.

Suddenly he said, "Victor, my brother, did you shine a
bright light in my face?"

"No, Claudio. No. Why do you ask?"

"Because, just at the moment when Jesus poured out His
Spirit upon me, I felt a light. That sounds strange. I didn't
see it. I felt it. It was very bright, and it seemed to fill the
room. Did you see it?"

"No," I said. "I didn't see it. But I, too, felt it. It must
have been Jesus Himself, right in this room."

We all rejoiced together.

Little did we know of the blessings and the persecutions
that were soon to come.

6

Signs and Wonders

We had never before seen the power of the Holy Spirit in action as we were seeing now. Every place we preached, people would come to Jesus in great numbers. And despite some of the controversy, many new believers were finding greater depth in the Lord than ever before.

As I read and reread the Book of Acts, I realized that God was indeed pouring out Himself upon His Church today, and that we were seeing results that compared with the New Testament account.

Something troubled me, though.

In Mark 16:17, 18, Christ told His disciples about the signs that would follow "them that believe." And He listed five of them. Up till this time, we had only experienced one of them.

So I talked to the brothers about it.

And, together, we talked to the Lord about it. Before long, we began seeing the results we prayed for. This next demonstration of Jesus' power had to do with casting out demons. This was something totally new to us. But if God's Word was to be taken at face value, and we believed it should be, then we could expect to see His power at work.

Near the church where Claudio was pastoring at this time was the village of La Guaripa. I had been there twice to preach, but they rejected us. They threw sticks and stones at us and did the same to every group that attempted to evangelize them.

Claudio and I believed the people could be reached, but we didn't know how. Then one day Claudio heard about the village's crazy woman. "Is she really crazy?" he asked.

"Yes," he was told. "She's been crazy for eight years."

"Eight years?"

"Si. She is so bad that they have to keep her chained up all the time."

He could hardly believe what he'd heard. "Chained up? Out in the jungle?"

"Oh, no. They keep her in a room. She is so bad they keep chains on her all the time."

Then someone asked Claudio, "Could God heal this woman?"

Claudio said, "I know God can heal her."

"Will He heal her?" was the next question.

"If it will bring glory to Him, I believe God will do it." Then he thought to himself that this might be the way the village could be reached.

"I would like to see that crazy woman," Claudio said. "Bring her to me."

"That would be difficult. She is violent. They can't release her."

"Then leave the chains on her and bring her in a canoe."

They were doubtful. "It might work. She is very strong."

"If you have to leave her chained, then do it. But I would like to see her."

A while later, they brought her. When they arrived at the dock, one of the men said, "See her; she is crazy. She is also very angry. She didn't want to come."

Claudio said, "Bring her to me."

When he looked at her, Claudio told me, he could see something was very wrong with her. Her hair was straggly and dirty, as if it hadn't been washed for a long time. Her clothes were in rags and scarcely covered her body. Her hands were like claws, very dirty, nails long and broken.

But he said it was her eyes that made him feel she was indeed possessed by a demon.

When he looked into those eyes, Claudio said he could see another spirit beside her own living inside the woman. The words she spoke were unintelligible. They sounded more like growling sounds deep in her throat than words.

Claudio said, "Release her."

"We can't! She's too strong. We're afraid."

"In the name of the Lord Jesus, release her!" he commanded.

So they loosed her from her chains. Then she stood in front of him, trembling. She spoke, and he could understand her words. "Because of you, they brought me here." It sounded like a challenge, some kind of accusation.

He said, "I have had you brought here to be healed."

She glared at him and began making strange noises again.

"You must be quiet. Change your attitude. Sit down quietly."

Immediately she obeyed. Claudio knew that that in itself was a miracle.

"Now," he said to the believers who were with him, "we are going to pray."

They prayed for three days. And on the third day she was healed. She was released from the demon that had possessed her. Suddenly she was the woman they had known before: calm, sweet. She went with the women, and they helped her get cleaned up. When Claudio saw her next, she was quiet and serene, and the wild, possessed look in her eyes was gone.

"God has done this," he told them. "He did it for a purpose: that you will all believe in Him, that you will believe that He has all power, that He, and He alone, can change your lives."

Many people heard about the woman's healing, and they came from everywhere to see for themselves. Even her parents, who were not believers, came to see the miracle of release. Because of her healing, this woman received Jesus. Also, her parents and many other people from her village accepted Him.

Today there is a strong, growing congregation of believers in the village of La Guaripa.

When we heard of this crazy woman's release from demon possession, we rejoiced. I thought, "Soon there will be other miracles and signs." And I was right.

I told the Lord, "You have allowed us to speak with new tongues and enabled us to cast out a demon. What are You going to do among us next?"

As usual, it wasn't long before the Lord showed us.

One day I was praying with Manuel Sena in Corozalito, when something happened that was entirely new to me, something that forced me to recognize the power of the devil. While we were praying, Manuel stiffened. His face took on a distant, otherworldly appearance. It frightened me. I started to speak to him, but before I said a word he began talking.

I hardly recognized his voice. It had changed. Even the expression on his face had changed and had taken on a twisted, demonic look.

Manuel's lips moved, and words came from his mouth, but it wasn't my friend who was speaking. The voice said, "You think Manuel's life belongs to God, don't you?"

Without waiting for an answer, the voice laughed, a cracked, hellish sound. "Well, you are wrong. Part of it belongs to me. I control him through the *secreto*."

I knew that Manuel had been a witch doctor before his conversion, and I knew he must have made use of a secreto, or fetish, quite often. It was an object of worship or "good luck," such as a feather, stone, or object of wood. Suddenly I realized I was face-to-face with one of the demons Manuel had known. This demon still exercised some control over my friend.

I challenged the voice, "You say Manuel has a secreto? You are wrong."

Again the harsh laugh. "No, I am not wrong. *You* are wrong! He has a secreto in his house."

In my heart I prayed, "Lord, please give me power over this demon."

Instantly I remembered that the power that was in me through the Holy Spirit was greater than that of the devil. And I was no longer afraid.

"Tell me where it is in his house," I commanded.

A sly look came to Manuel's face. "Oh, no, you don't. You can't make me tell you. You'll have to find that out for yourself."

Suddenly, as suddenly as Manuel's appearance had changed, the awful look, the demonic presence was gone. Manuel relaxed and smiled at me, and I knew he had not been aware of the trance or the conversation. I decided to deal directly with him.

"Manuel, I must ask you this. Since you've become a believer, have you practiced witchcraft?"

He shook his head, a hurt look on his face. "No, Victor."

"Then why have you kept that secreto in your house?"

Manuel's face turned pale. "How did you know?"

I told him of my confrontation with the demon.

Shamefacedly, he said, "Yes, Victor. I kept just that one. It seemed harmless. . . ."

"It isn't harmless, my brother. The demons are still using you. And they will continue to use you as long as you keep that secreto."

He bowed his head. "I'm sorry, Victor. Will you pray that I will be released from the secreto's power?"

"Yes. We must gather some others to pray. But before we do, tell me, where is the secreto?"

He described the fetish, which he kept wrapped in a

cloth, inside a glass jar, and both locked in a box.

As we gathered around Manuel and prayed, we were beset by a terrible presence, as if the devil himself was resisting us. We prayed for a long time, and finally we felt the power of the devil was destroyed and Manuel set free.

One of the brothers said, "God has shown me that you, Victor, must go to Manuel's house with him. Then you must destroy the secreto."

Since his house was about ten kilometers distance, we decided to stay in Corozalito overnight. The next morning, Manuel, his son Francisco, and I arose early to go to Manuel's house.

When we arrived there, Manuel's daughter-in-law, Ana Monteroso de Sena, told us a remarkable story. Approximately at the same time we were praying in Corozalito, Manuel's dog seemed to go crazy. He suddenly rushed into the house, barking furiously, as though being pursued.

"When he came in," Ana said, "I was seized with fear. A terrible presence of some kind came into the house with him."

"What did you do?" I asked.

"I crawled up on my bed and prayed. I was so afraid. Then the dog went out of the room and that terrible presence left, too."

I turned to Manuel, "Show me the secreto."

He took me into the very room where Ana had prayed. He found the box and opened it. He gasped in surprise, "The secreto is gone!"

"Gone? But you have the box."

He showed me the cloth in which the fetish had been wrapped. Instead of the fetish, there was nothing but a little mound of powder. It was gone, disintegrated.

Once again we praised God for His marvelous power which was able to put demons to flight and to destroy their works.

During those days, the church had commissioned a group of us to go out to other churches that needed to be strengthened. As Claudio said, "We went to the ones which were suffering from tired blood."

We would sing and preach and teach. Most of the time, God would bring new life to them. One of those churches was just outside the village of Magangue. Many people came to Jesus there.

God also did some remarkable miracles there.

That first night we talked about healing, about how we believed Jesus was able to do among us today all He had done when He was on earth. We really believed this, though we had seen very few of the miracles we longed to see.

During the service one night, a man said, "My wife needs to be healed."

As he was still speaking I felt God was going to heal that woman, even before he named the problem.

"She has cancer," he said. "She's been operated on four times. And now she's ready to go back to the clinic at Barranquilla for the fifth surgery."

He spoke to his wife, and she stood up with great difficulty. "She also has arthritis. She can't move her shoulders or arms. Our little girl has to bathe and dress her."

"What is your wife's name?"

"Her name is Chica Cruz."

"Bring her to me."

Every eye was on the woman as she painfully made her way to the front. Some of our group gathered around her. We put our hands on her, as Jesus had done, and as Peter had done. "In the name of Jesus Christ, be healed!" I said. And I *felt* the power of God. *I actually felt it!*

The woman, Chica, was instantly healed! Right then she began moving her arms and shoulders, something she hadn't been able to do for years.

In gratitude, her husband lifted his hands and praised God. In fact, the whole church praised God. I praised God, too. For we were now beginning to see more of the signs Jesus described.

The next afternoon our group gathered for special prayer. "We must ask God for His special anointing upon us," Calixto said, "because now He is beginning to use us to heal."

It was a very blessed time.

That night we prayed for Chica, asking God to complete her healing, to remove the cancer. When she went home that night, she expelled the cancer. It was very large. From that time on she was free of the symptoms, and she has been a powerful witness for the Lord.

Largely because of her witness, the church at Magangue began to experience unusual growth. Chica has since become pastor of the church at La Sabana de Beltron that came into being because of her dynamic ministry.

In the same service that night, there was a man with tuberculosis. He had been in the hospital, but they could do nothing for him, so he had come home to die.

I saw him while I was praying for some of the others. When I came close to him, he held out his hands to me, trembling. He was so very thin and frail. Since he was tubercular, I wanted to give him some special attention. I told him, "Stay here a moment. I will be right back."

After I had prayed for some others, I asked Calixto and the rest of the group to come with me to pray for the tubercular man. I laid my hands upon him, and he trembled very much. I said, "Will you come up to the front of the church?"

"Why? For what reason?" he asked.

"So we can all get around you as we pray."

He shook his head. "No, I can't. I'm too bad. I'm so bad I don't think God can heal me. It's too late."

It was then that I commanded, "In the name of Jesus, be healed!"

A look of surprise spread across his face. He stood up, totally healed! The next day he went to the market, bought a bag of groceries, and carried them home by himself: this man that had been given up for dead.

In the New Testament, Jesus healed even those who didn't believe in Him. And we saw this happen at Magangue.

It happened to an old man who had suffered eight years

with arthritis. He had been rich and had spent one hundred fifty thousand pesos (approximately $7,500 U.S.) for treatment. But nothing helped him. He had to be carried every place he went.

This man's friends brought him to the church that night. He didn't really want to come, because he was a nonbeliever.

He was in much pain when I saw him. His arms were stuck to his sides, and he couldn't move them. He could just barely walk.

I said to Calixto and Gregorio, "Let's pray for the man with arthritis."

They agreed. We laid our hands on him and prayed. Immediately he was able to move his body a little better. His shoulders loosened up a bit. He wasn't completely healed just then, but as his friends were carrying him out of the church, his legs and arms were suddenly released from the arthritis. And by the time he got to his car, he was normal.

He was so excited; he was like a little boy. He said, "I can't keep all this good news to myself. I'm going to tell everybody!"

He ran up the steps to the church and began shouting, "Look, everybody. I'm healed! I'm healed!"

He ripped open his shirt and removed it. "See, I haven't been able to do this for eight years!" He embraced a fifteen-year-old girl who was beside him. She was startled, but happy. "Daughter, God has healed me! I haven't been able to even move my arms for many years!"

He was filled with such joy as I had seldom seen.

After the service, I went to the man's house. When he saw me at the door, he invited me in. The house was filled with people, society people and government people. "Come in! Come in!" he said.

Turning to the crowd, he told them, "Come and meet the man who prayed for me!" He presented me to them all.

I was reminded of Acts 10, when Peter was in the house of Cornelius. And I thought, "This is my opportunity to talk to all of them." So, with the power and confidence of the Holy Spirit, I told them of the miracles of God: how He could change a man's life as well as heal a man's body.

One of the representatives of Congress, who was there, invited me to his home. I went that same hour and spoke with him. He asked me to pray for him, and I did. He opened his heart and received Jesus Christ. His wife asked me to come and speak to a group of women, which I did a few days later. There were seventy women present, and I shared the love and healing of Jesus with them.

All of this was brought about through the healing of the arthritic man.

Not long after these miraculous incidents in Magangue, I was on my way to Puerto Libertador. On the way I stopped at Planeta Rica, where Octavio, my brother-in-law, was pastor. As I prepared to leave, Octavio said, "Please stay till tomorrow."

"Of course," I said, and stayed. I wondered what the Lord might be planning to do.

That very evening, my question was answered when

some people from the community came to tell us about a man who was dying from a heart attack. He had been ill with a heart problem for many years. The next morning, when we arrived at his home, the whole family had gathered.

The man was stretched out on his bed, surrounded by many people. His doctor had told the family to gather, because death was very close. When we arrived, the dying man appeared to be dead already. He was cold and appeared to have no pulse.

The day before, a member of the family had asked, "Shall we send for the priest so you can make your final confession?"

"No!" he had answered. "I want you to bring me an evangelical pastor. He can help me."

That was when they had sent for us.

We tried to talk to the dying man, but he was almost unconscious and could neither hear nor understand us. He was so weak he couldn't talk.

So Octavio and I knelt beside the bed and prayed. We anointed his body with oil. Then we laid our hands on his chest and head.

"Lord," we prayed, "we ask you to raise this man up."

After we had prayed for him, we left him alone for a few minutes. Then someone noticed the man's body was warm. "He has a fever! This must be the end."

The warmth was life returning to a body that was practically dead. The man began coughing, and within an hour he could sit up by himself.

This man who had been given up for dead was now alive. God had done the impossible!

Just as we had asked Him, God began to fulfill all the signs He promised. And now we had seen three of the five.

7

Living by Faith

After pastoring the church at Corozalito for about three years, I felt the Lord leading me to evangelize in other areas. Many still had not heard the Gospel. So I prayed, and the church prayed, and we felt the Holy Spirit was sending me out. It was agreed then, and Calixto remained in Corozalito to be the leader for the church.

The various congregations agreed to try to pay me two hundred pesos. Then, of course, I would have some time to work on my farm and earn a little bit more. This arrangement didn't work out very well, though, because some of the congregations failed to send me their money.

That left me in serious financial trouble, because I had given myself completely to evangelization and hadn't planted any yucca or bananas during all that time.

To make matters worse, both my house and the church burned down. So I had no money, no savings, no crops, and now no home. Some people, including missionary Bob Reed, came and helped me to rebuild my house. That was good, but I still had no money.

My situation got so bad that I didn't have enough money even to buy salt. I had to work in the bakery to earn a little money. But for a day's work—a long, hot day—I could only make three pesos.

So I asked Maria de Amante, Calixto's wife, "Is it true that Doña Victoria is looking for workers?"

Maria said, "I don't know. But I will find out."

Maria sent a messenger to Doña Victoria's large plantation, and her answer came back on Saturday. "Yes. You can work for me next week. I need help to clear more land."

Sunday I thought about it. "Doña Victoria will pay me for a whole week. And I need the money. She will be faithful and pay me for what I am worth. And that will be good."

She needed somebody to chop down trees and clear land. I could do that, for I had done that kind of work many times before. Then I thought, "But Doña Victoria can get many people to work for her. The Lord has very few to work for Him." That made me feel uneasy.

I asked the Lord what I should do. It became clear that He wanted me to trust Him. So on faith I sent word to Doña Victoria, "Don't wait for me on Monday. I'm not coming. I'm going to go work for the Lord."

So on Monday I went to work for the Lord. And that work was to evangelize every person I came across on the road, no matter who he was.

That was my decision, because when you go out to cut down trees, you cut down every tree that's in your path. I was going out to work for the Lord. So I was going to cut everything, evangelize everybody, that I came across.

When I left Corozalito, I met many on the road. And I talked to all of them about Jesus. That first night I arrived at a little house and found many believers there. So we talked about Jesus and had a blessed time. Early in the morning I started to leave.

The lady of the house said, "Brother, are you going to leave without eating breakfast?"

I said, "I will eat something along the way." I didn't know how I could do this, because I didn't have any money.

She said, "Look, I have three pesos. Take them so you can get something to eat."

I had walked only about three kilometers when I came to the house of a believer who told me he had two sick children. I stopped and prayed for them, then prepared to leave.

He said, "Brother, you must eat breakfast with us." So I ate breakfast with him.

I left his house and was soon in the thick jungle. After just a little while, I heard someone behind me shouting, "Brother Victor! Brother Victor!"

I turned and looked. At first I saw nobody. Then I saw one of the children of the family with whom I had just eaten breakfast. He had run a long way. When he caught up I asked him, "What happened? Is someone ill? Did someone die?"

He said, "No. I have something I want to give you," and handed me ten pesos. I thanked him and went on my way toward Libertador, praising God.

That day I arrived in Libertador. I spent the rest of the day there, and we had a church service that night. I helped the brothers and shared the Word with them. The next day

I went to Pimienta. At Pimienta I spent the evening with the believers, reading the Scriptures and praising God.

The next day, after having been gone just a little over three days, I arrived home in Corozalito. I had left home with nothing in my pocket. Now I had thirteen pesos. So, I concluded, the Lord pays better wages than even Doña Victoria.

I had tested God again, and He had proven Himself to me.

So I decided to dedicate myself to work for the Lord the whole year in the same way. I would give Him at least half my time. And for my efforts, I wouldn't accept anything from the church, only from the Lord.

I figured that I needed 300 pesos each month to care for my living expenses. So I told the Lord I would keep track of everything that came to me, both money and gifts. I would figure the worth of the gifts and count that amount the same as cash. In one column in my book I would record that income, and in another column I would figure my total expenses.

During all of this time, I would not communicate any of my needs to anyone. I believed the Lord, who knew my needs, would touch the hearts of others, and they would give accordingly.

And so I began. On one side of the page I kept track of my time: one month would be fifteen days, another month, ten days, and so on. On the other side of the page I kept track of the monies (in cash and gifts) I received from the Lord. When I had worked a total of thirty days for the Lord,

I would total up my account of returns from the Lord. I always found that the Lord had paid me more than the 300 pesos I needed.

In other words, the Lord would always keep ahead of me. He would advance me money before I needed it. Throughout the year He did this, always keeping ahead of me. He was never in debt to me: I was always in debt to Him.

I had tested the Lord in a measurable way. And I learned to my own satisfaction what a good administrator and provider He is.

By the time the year was over, I knew for sure I could trust God to do everything He had promised. During the time I had lived and worked with the people at Corozalito, I had been teaching complete trust in God. Now they could see, as I, that He could be totally trusted.

One day I asked, "Do you want God to bless you?"

"Yes, we do," they answered.

"Do you want God to continue healing you?"

"Yes—of course."

"Do you want to continue to see all these other miracles among us? As He has been showing us?"

Again the answer was yes. I reminded them of the time I had been so sick. I had told God if He would heal me I would do anything for Him. "That was when the Lord raised me up," I said. "I am so grateful that I now go everywhere telling people about the wonderful things Jesus does."

The people responded in ways that surprised me.

One man came to me and said, "I want to pattern my life after the people in the early Church."

"That's good."

"Then I want to give my farm to the church. I will sell it and give the proceeds to the church."

Someone else soon came to me and said the same thing.

At first that sounded like a good idea. Then I thought, *What would happen if every believer did that? What would happen? How would we work? How would we live? We'd soon have nothing.*

So we all began to search the Bible to see if this offer was scriptural. When we couldn't find any Scripture to support this kind of act, we agreed it was not best. So we all decided we would seek other ways to obey the Lord.

All of us were so very much in earnest in our desire to live for God that we examined our hearts and lives every day. We spent time in fasting and praying, putting the Word of God in our lives as best we could.

God began to do some new things in our lives then, working in us in practical, measurable ways. We kept records of how we did. During one meeting a man came in and said, "This week the Lord helped me not to become angry." We wrote it down.

Another man said, "This week I was able to go the whole time without lying." We wrote that down.

"I was able to cut down on my lying to just three or four times," someone else said.

We would confess our faults to one another. We would then praise the Lord together for the ways He was able to grow in our lives. As we lived this way we began to have revival.

One night we so felt God's presence that we prayed for five hours without even knowing it. The time seemed like minutes instead of hours. The whole place was illuminated that night, filled with the presence of God. We all felt it, though we couldn't adequately describe it.

That was a wonderful night. We laid hands on one another to receive the fullness of the Holy Spirit. Some who had not received gifts from the Holy Spirit before received them. Some were given power to heal.

And all of us had real, inward power from the Holy Spirit that night. This became evident when someone brought me a young girl who was acting strangely.

Suddenly she became wild. She acted crazy. And we were scared of her. Just then the Lord told me, "This girl is possessed of an evil spirit. If you pray for her, she will be released."

So we laid hands on her and prayed. Immediately she was set free. We were excited and joyful. We praised God for her release. The girl left the meeting happy, content, and normal.

These were the days when Juan Gonzalez and some others, including myself, were filled with the Holy Spirit. The word spread that God was doing mighty miracles among His people at Corozalito. And people from everywhere began coming to us as they had come to Jesus: the sick, the lame, the blind, the poor in spirit. And the power of God would heal them and fill them. A constant procession of people came to Corozalito from many villages all around the area. Often the people were healed during the preaching, and we wouldn't even know about it till later.

So many people came to us that we hardly had time to eat or sleep.

It was then that the devil began his work among us. Because of the outpouring of the Holy Spirit, some of the churches said, "All that's happening at Corozalito is the work of the devil. It isn't God at all."

I couldn't understand their reasoning. People were coming to us, and their lives were being changed. People were being healed of all manner of sickness. They were meeting God. Persecution began to come. It hurt us and confused us.

One night we were together in a house, praying around the table.

Suddenly I felt myself suspended high above the earth. I didn't know how it had happened, or what was really happening. But I was so high in the air that I was afraid to look down.

It was one of my first visions.

I saw thousands of people involved in this great movement, this great time of blessing from God. I could see the extent of it. I could see people coming to us from far away. I could see myself in the middle of it all.

Then I saw the devil begin to confuse people. Some said, "Let's cut them off, the church at Corozalito. They're not of the Lord. They're of the devil."

In my vision I said, "No! No, no! That's impossible. You

can't cut us off. It is wrong. This is what God wants! This is His will!"

When I opened my eyes, I was back in the house, still at the table. The others were there. But in some miraculous way I had been gone from them for a while. And I didn't understand it.

Somehow, through what I had seen, I knew there was soon going to be a time of dissension, when Satan would try to destroy us.

The outpouring of the Holy Spirit had come upon us so quickly, so powerfully, that we were unprepared to handle it. No one among us had had any exposure to Pentecostalism. None of us had even heard of speaking in tongues, except in the New Testament.

Some, like Juan Gonzalez, talked very little about the experience. Others made much of it and talked about it constantly. With so little knowledge, we were bound to make some mistakes, and we did.

One mistake was the emphasis some of the brothers placed on some of the gifts, especially speaking in tongues. A few went so far as to declare that this particular gift was the indispensable sign, the indisputable evidence of the filling of the Holy Spirit.

Along with Calixto, Gregorio, and a few others, I did not agree. It was true that a number of us had received this gift. It was also true that some who had experienced this phenomenon were being unusually used of God in preaching. We could not deny this fact. But some were not, and Juan was one of them.

Again and again, Gregorio, Calixto, and I were driven to

our knees and into the Scriptures. We knew we must find God's mind, His definite directions and leading in this matter. In our searching, though we noted several places where the disciples spoke in tongues, we found no indication that this gift was to be the universal sign or seal of the Holy Spirit's indwelling presence.

On occasion, our services became bedlam, with several brothers and sisters desiring to use their new gift at once. There were times when I rebuked people who seemed to exceed the limits of Paul's command in 1 Corinthians 14 that everything be done "decently and in order."

We were very grateful for the calm, sane guidance given to us by some of the LAM missionaries, particularly Bob Reed and David Howard.

But we were troubled when we detected counterfeit gifts of the Spirit; some excessive emotion; and an overemphasis upon speaking in tongues, the casting out of demons, and other physical manifestations.

It was during the high tide of this activity that we invited David Howard to be our Easter-week speaker at Corozalito. The year was 1963. Apparently the devil tried to prevent David from coming. Because, only days before he was to come, he was stricken with a sudden, rather severe illness.

"I had no fever," he told me. "But I had chills and diarrhea. I was confined to bed and could hardly move for five days. I didn't think I could possibly make the trip."

However, God impressed upon him the importance of coming. "I felt my illness was nothing but satanic opposition," David told me when he arrived at Corozalito. "So, by a step of faith, I declared that with Jesus' help I was going to go."

He said he had suffered with diarrhea for five days straight, right up till the moment he stepped on board the bus. He told the Lord, "I'm doing this because I believe it is in obedience to You. So You're going to have to take over."

And God did. David had no more trouble from the time he left his home in Cartagena, all the way to Corozalito, through Easter week, until he arrived back home.

We were praying that through David's ministry among us, God would settle differences, calm disputes, heal bodies and families, and pour Himself out upon us in His own unique, sovereign way. It was a huge order, but we were trusting Him to do all that.

On the way to Corozalito, David had to spend a night on the trail. Because of some of the goings-on at our village, he was fearful of being with us. He confided this to the Lord. The next morning, when he opened his Bible, David's eyes were immediately drawn to these words:

> For the Lord God will help me; therefore I shall not be confounded: therefore have I set my face like a flint, and I know that I shall not be ashamed.
>
> Isaiah 50:7

As he related this to me, David said, "Clearly God was telling me: 'This is My promise for you for this time, for these days.' And from that moment, I went through the entire week with a light heart and a spring to my step."

It's a good thing God did prepare David.

For, just a day or so before the special meetings of Easter week, something happened that set the whole community to buzzing. A man arrived in Corozalito and made a startling and disturbing announcement. "I am a prophet," he said. "God has sent me to you."

8

Some Stumbling Blocks

"You're a prophet?" I asked the man.

"Yes. God has sent me to Corozalito. He's given me a new and special word for the people gathered here this week."

I wasn't impressed with the man, though many of the people were. I asked Calixto what he thought. He shrugged his shoulders. "I am not sure," he said. "I know the people would like to hear from a prophet. Maybe God sent one—maybe not."

Gregorio's response was somewhat the same. "If God has sent him, okay. But if not . . . ," and he shrugged.

We left the man alone, though we kept an eye on him.

When David Howard arrived, we told him about the prophet.

David didn't say much, though I could tell he wasn't exactly pleased.

Just before the first service, David said, "I haven't seen the prophet since I came. Where is he?"

"He's out in the woods getting a special word from God."

David raised his eyebrows. I could tell he was a little nervous. So was I, because I feared some sort of confrontation between the missionary and the prophet.

The prophet came into the service while David was preaching. He timed it right. Everybody noticed him. He ambled up to the front and sat in the first row. I sat where I could watch him. David kept an eye on him, though he said nothing to acknowledge the man's presence.

During the service, the prophet began rocking back and forth, rolling his eyes back into his head. He breathed so heavily that I could hear him from where I was.

Immediately after the service, the prophet made his move.

He approached David, grabbed both his arms, and moved him back against the wall of the church.

I was nervous, but there was nothing I could do.

The prophet had David cornered against the wall. Breathing heavily, he stared deep into David's eyes.

David appeared relaxed. He didn't speak, but very calmly looked the man in the eye.

The prophet shoved his face close to David's and said, "Brother, have you ever seen God heal a man?"

David smiled and said, "Yes, of course. I've seen God heal several people."

"Well, have you heard about the new word of prophecy God is giving for this week?"

"I heard there was something going on," and he sort of smiled. "What can you tell me?"

"I was out in the woods today. And God has given me a special message for this week."

Suddenly I began to wonder if this man really was a

prophet. He may have sensed that here was a chance to get a large following from the more than six hundred people who had come to Corozalito for the week. So he was publicly challenging David to a power struggle.

The people couldn't know all that was at stake. David Howard's teaching from the Word was clearly anointed by God. But this prophet had a charisma that the Colombians could respond to. The prophet knew this and tried to capitalize on it.

David was poised and calm. "Well, what is your new and special word from the Lord?"

"I've got three words from the Lord."

"What are they?"

"They are new words from God for us today—today in Corozalito."

Those around us became very quiet. "The first word is that we need to love God more. We don't love Him enough."

David didn't answer.

"The second word is that we're in the last days, because there's a lot of apostasy. And God told me that in the last days there would be a lot of apostasy. So the coming of the Lord is very near."

Again David didn't answer.

The prophet raised his hands dramatically. "And the third word from the Lord is—is. . . ." A puzzled look came to his face. He scratched his head in bewilderment. Then he mumbled, "Well, I can't remember it at the moment."

I knew that if David failed this test, the prophet would

take over the crowd, despite anything Calixto, Gregorio, and I could do.

But David didn't hesitate. He shot right back: "Don't tell me those are new words from God. God gave the first word to Moses three thousand five hundred years ago when He gave him the Ten Commandments. He said, 'Thou shalt love the Lord thy God with all thine heart.' There's nothing new about that. You didn't get a new word from God on that one!"

Every eye was on the prophet, but he didn't speak.

David went on, "And it's been two thousand years since the New Testament told us that in the latter days there would be apostasy before the coming of the Lord. There's nothing new about that. Don't tell me that's a new word from God."

David then gave his parting shot. "You can't even remember the third one yourself. So don't talk to me about new revelations from God!"

Then David turned and walked away. I thanked God for the words of wisdom He had given him for this critical moment.

The prophet didn't say anything either. He turned and slipped through the crowd, and I didn't see any more of him that night. Throughout the week, though, he was very much in evidence.

On the final morning, the prophet made such a disturbance, right at the beginning of the service, that Calixto escorted him out. But he was back in a few minutes, sitting in the front row. He acted normally for a little while. But when David got to an important part of his message, he started in again. The man was clever. He didn't act up enough for Calixto to throw him out again, but just enough to draw attention to himself.

I think by now the people were getting pretty tired of his disturbances. I know I was.

During the final prayers, just before the final hymn, the prophet made his last effort to take over. But he'd already gone too far, and his scheme backfired. Our chapel seats at that time had no backs on them; they were just benches. The prophet was sitting on a front-row bench, as I said, and during the prayer, he began rolling his eyes back into his head again, raising his arms and rocking and swaying back and forth.

I was afraid the man might attempt to get up and take over.

Just as we started the final hymn, he toppled over backward and landed in the lap of the man behind him. He did it just as the song leader said, "We'll now stand for the closing hymn."

The man he fell on grabbed the prophet by the collar and said, "Stand up!" And he gave him a big shove.

The prophet stood up shakily. His arms were raised during the hymn, and his eyes were rolling. Finally he collapsed in a heap on the floor. I guess he thought this would be very dramatic and that people would gather round him, which would break up the service.

But that didn't happen. Nobody paid any attention to him.

When the song was ended, people walked past him, leaving him lying there, twitching.

Nobody spoke to him. They walked around him and left the chapel. When everybody had gone, the prophet got up, dusted himself off, and calmly walked out of the chapel, as though nothing had happened.

I was thankful that David Howard had confronted him the first night. If he hadn't, the false prophet might have been able to take over. The man left Corozalito that day and was never seen again.

Many wondered if he was the devil in human form. I can't say, though I believe he was possessed by the devil.

The whole episode was a good lesson to Calixto and me. We never forgot how cleverly Satan attempts to reveal himself as an angel of light.

I remember the day the Lord made it clear we were to meet at the church for a service of reconciliation. He told us to meet. He also told us the specific time we were to meet: six o'clock in the evening.

But we still had much to learn from the Lord.

We didn't listen to His commands that time. So instead of everybody being there, some did this, and some did that, some went here or there. But we weren't interested in being at the service when He told us to be.

Instead we decided that we would meet and plan our next evangelistic campaign. Well, when I got to the church that night, I began to see how it is when the Holy Spirit is not in control. He desires to control God's people. He gives us liberty—but not to walk in a lazy manner.

Later I realized that the Lord wanted to begin preparing me for a ministry of reconciliation.

But I didn't see any control in the meeting. I was not in control. Nobody was in control. God was not in control. There was a great lack, a great emptiness in the service. And I thought, *Why is this so?*

The next morning we found out. In devotions the Lord spoke to us through one of the sisters. "We have all sinned against the Holy Spirit. We have disobeyed Him."

"Why? How?" someone asked. "In what way have we disobeyed the Holy Spirit?"

"God told us to meet together at six o'clock last evening. And we didn't go as He told us to go. He gave us specific directions, a specific time. And we refused. We couldn't have been bothered. That could cause us to fail in the campaign."

The sister sat down. And a great sadness came to us. That was hard for us to take. Yet we knew it was true. We began weeping and threw ourselves down upon the ground to pray. It was a time of blessing, of pain, and of sorrow.

We prayed for a long time, asking God to forgive us.

After a while my brother Gregorio said, "It is all right now. I have seen the Lord. While we were praying, He appeared to me. He was signaling to us that it is all right now."

We began to rejoice and to minister to one another. Many verses from the Bible were given that had to do with consolation. We said to one another, "The next time God tells us to come at six o'clock, we will be there on time."

We knew He wanted us to be there by six o'clock that very evening. So we were all there. We came before six, most of us even missing our suppers to obey Him.

God met us in a special way that night, because we had obeyed Him. The exposition from the Word was precious. The time was glorious. God gave us His gifts that night: healing of bodies, healing of faith, the gift of love and prophecy. All of His gifts were manifest that night. All because we had obeyed Him in a simple thing.

And the result was that the campaign was successful. The church was full each time, and many came to know Jesus. The church grew so much that we had to build a larger one to hold all the people.

The lesson I learned was this: Out of our simple trusting, doing the thing that God told us to do, He enabled us to speak with all the power that He has. We were different when the Holy Spirit got hold of us, when we yielded ourselves completely to Him.

When that happens to one, God uses that person as a trumpet for Himself. And that's a very precious thing.

After this particular time of reconciliation and confession, as the people confessed their sins one to another, it became a time of great blessing. We went out to all the other villages around Corozalito and told what God had done. And the same kind of blessing came to them. We even went as far as Cartagena. And again, His blessings fell upon them as well.

Not long after this, God began calling me to go to Puerto Libertador. It happened in a praise celebration. At the time He spoke to me, the Puerto Libertador church had already been in a stagnant condition for several years.

Though the church was very small at that time, they were beset by divisions. One group was open to the moving of the Holy Spirit in their midst. The other group was totally opposed to the ministry of the Holy Spirit. Not knowing what to do, I immediately attempted to unite the two.

It was like trying to mix oil and water. They would not unite.

At first the church began to grow a little bit. Then for months it was stagnant again and ceased to grow.

Things came to a climax during a three-day youth retreat. During that time, I was speaking on the power and manifestations of the Holy Spirit. Some people interfered and told me to stop.

Seven people in all opposed me as I presented the ministry of the Holy Spirit. For a year and a half they resisted all my efforts and all the Holy Spirit's efforts.

Something had to happen.

And it did, in God's way and time, when one of the opposition came to me and asked, "How do you see the church? Is it in good condition, or not?"

I said, "It could be better."

"Some of the people are saying that you are destroying the church by teaching falsehood."

During this conversation I was praying in my heart for God to give me wisdom to answer him.

After telling me all the things that were wrong with the church, and with me, the pastor, he asked, "Do you have a solution for the church?"

"Yes," I said, "I have a solution—God's solution."

"What is it?"

"Do you know what God says about a *casa*, a house, that is divided? Do you remember that the Bible says that such a house will fail? That it cannot prevail?"

"Yes, I know that," he said. "So we have to unite ourselves."

"Exactly."

"But it is impossible for us to unite ourselves as long as you are teaching the present power and manifestations of the Holy Spirit. While you do that, we cannot unite ourselves."

I said, "There is another solution."

"What is it?"

"There are two groups in the church. The church must decide to follow one of those groups. For that to happen, the other group must submit to their leadership."

"How could that work?" he asked.

"One group must decide what they feel is the direction for the church to go. And since the church cannot go both directions, then the other group must drop out."

He thought a minute. "I agree with you. We will have a church meeting, and the whole church will decide which group to follow."

Since he was the spokesman for the opposing seven, and since all of them were church officials, he thought they would be able to persuade the entire church to go their way. But that was not God's plan. When the church met, the majority decided to follow the Holy Spirit's leading.

Reluctantly, the seven said they would drop out of leadership for a time. They hoped and believed that the church would fail without them. But it did not. Instead it immediately prospered.

Finally after over a year and a half, I was now able to put together a truly spiritual program. God began pouring out His rich love and warmth to the church. It was beautiful what He did. People began flocking to the church. So many came that we often had no more room for them.

Nearly every day someone came to me and said, *Hermano* Victor, Brother Victor, isn't there a study tonight?"

I'd say, "No, there was one last night. There will be one tomorrow night. But not tonight."

"Look, Pastor," he'd say, "I came to give myself to the Lord tonight."

I'd say, "Good. Let's go!"

So I'd go over and open the church. Each time this happened, they would open their hearts to the Lord, and He would become Lord of their lives.

During my time at the church at Puerto Libertador, whenever someone came to the Lord, I gave them a card telling the date of their decision. I would also keep a copy. This helped us to see the way God was working among His people.

When I first went to the church, there were only about fifteen baptized members. When I left, at the end of two years, there were one hundred sixty. Most of these came to know the Lord during the last six months.

9

The All-Sufficient Saviour

In our part of Colombia, snakebites are greatly feared, because they cause so many deaths. So, when Maria de Amante, Calixto's wife, was bitten by a poisonous snake, we were very concerned.

Even though we immediately gathered around her and began praying, Maria's foot and leg had already begun to swell. Her face was very pale. "It hurts awfully," she said. "It hurts all the way up my side, clear up to my shoulder."

As I prayed, I felt a strange power come into my body. It was different from anything I had ever felt before. I laid my hand on Maria's foot where the fang marks were.

Almost at once, Maria opened her eyes.

"The pain," she said in astonishment. "The pain—it's leaving. It feels as if it's draining down from my shoulder, down my arm, down my side, and out my foot."

To our delight, she was healed almost instantly. Within minutes she was up on her feet, walking and praising God. Just to be sure she was all right, Calixto sent for a doctor. When he came the next day and examined Maria carefully, he looked disgusted.

"You owe me fifty pesos," he said. "That's to teach you not to be so *bobo*, so foolish, again as to call a doctor when he's not needed."

Despite the high cost for his services, we rejoiced over the miracle of Maria's healing.

Simona de Landero, my sister-in-law, was walking one Sunday near a stream. She was bitten by a very large, poisonous snake. She fell into the water and would have drowned, but her young son lifted her head out of the water and rested it on a rock.

As she lay there, very weak and ill, the snake crawled closer to her.

Simona said, "I command you, in the name of Jesus, to stay there so the men can come and kill you!"

Instantly, the snake stopped moving.

Simona was very weak by this time, but she got up and sat by a tree till a man and woman happened to come by. She described the situation and asked them to kill the snake and then take her home. This they did.

Then they sent her son to the church and asked us to pray for her. During the time of prayer, there was a message given in tongues. The interpretation that immediately followed was: "God wishes to glorify Himself through this incident. He is going to do a miracle and heal this woman. . . ."

As a result of the message and the interpretation, we sent a group to bring her to the church. We gathered around her, laid our hands upon her, and prayed for the healing the Lord had promised. Again there was another message and interpretation. This time the word was: "I am the Lord. I am your Doctor, your Physician. I will heal this woman. . . ."

I decided not to send for a doctor.

My decision caused much discussion in the church.

Someone said, "You should get a doctor."

"The Lord promised to be the Doctor," I said. "He said He would come and heal her."

"But she might die. . . ."

"God said He would heal her," I said.

"If she dies, we will denounce you and report you to the law. . . ."

". . . then you would go to jail."

Those of us who believed the message we had been given said, "Fine. We'll take that chance."

Simona did well the rest of that day. She was all right Monday, Tuesday, and even Wednesday. The only thing that happened was that she would drain black, very black blood from the bite. Some of the brothers said, "Let's pray that the blood will stop."

I said, "We should let it come out. It's bad blood. The poison is coming out." But they insisted, so we prayed, and the bleeding stopped. Immediately we saw that was wrong, because her body developed black blotches where the poison blood clotted in her veins.

Her condition worsened, and we feared she would die. Her fever increased and got very high. She began to hallucinate and didn't know us when we spoke to her. Suddenly I was filled with doubts.

In that condition I lay down and talked to the Lord. "Perhaps I should have gotten a doctor," I said. "Maybe she will die. Then it will be my fault. . . ."

As I was talking to the Lord, I fell asleep with the heavy burden of my doubts on my mind. I guess I dreamed, but God spoke to me. I saw two figures kneeling. One was named Truth and the other was Doubt.

Truth spoke first: "Simona will not die."

"Simona is going to die," Doubt answered.

"It is a lie," Truth said.

Back and forth they argued. And it seemed that I was just listening to them, watching them, not knowing which one to believe. Then Truth began quoting verses from the Bible: "Whatsoever ye shall ask in my name, that will I do. . . . every one that asketh receiveth. . . ."

With that I got up and said, "Doubt, you don't have any reason for being here. Simona won't die, because we prayed for her according to the promises of God!"

Then I walked back and forth, praying and quoting Bible verses, praising God for healing my sister-in-law. I reprimanded Doubt in the name of Jesus, and accepted Simona's healing in Jesus' name. A few minutes later, I was filled with peace and returned to the church.

We prayed together and asked the Lord what it was He was trying to show us through this incident. The Lord showed us that the "commissioned group" (select evangelists and preachers) must become more united. Immediately we began to make peace with one another.

Some of the things that came up—some of the things we held against one another—seemed to be so trivial, so minor. But when something is preventing you from having God's complete blessing, then it's not trivial or small. One by one, we opened our hearts to one another, asked forgiveness of one another, and asked God to purify and cleanse us.

What a time of blessing that was.

We were united again, fully reconciled. We wept and rejoiced together. Then the Lord said, "Now you may anoint Simona again and pray for her, and I will heal her."

So we did.

With great joy and humility, we anointed Simona again. With tears of rejoicing, we prayed that God would raise her up. And He did as He promised. Within three days she was walking the streets, praising God for His wonderful goodness to her.

We, the "commissioned group," thanked God for the lesson He had taught us, and we continued to walk with the Lord.

Another remarkable miracle of healing took place in Chinu. I was there with the group, preaching in a campaign. It was five in the afternoon, and we were very tired, since we had gotten up very early and had been teaching and preaching all day. We hadn't even taken time to eat or rest.

We noticed a man and a burro stop on the road nearby. A woman who appeared to be weak or sick was riding the burro.

They stopped and talked with some people. And we saw them point toward us, but we couldn't hear what they were saying. The man nodded and said something, then turned and came to us. He greeted me, then said, "My wife cannot stand. Her legs are paralyzed. She must sit down or lie down all the time. She has been that way for four years."

I didn't say anything, and he continued, "We are on our way to visit a new doctor. We have been to many doctors. They all say there is nothing they can do for her."

He pointed toward the men he had been talking with. "They said to come to you, and you would heal her."

"Some of the people told you not to come to me, didn't they?" I asked, for there had seemed to be some disagreement among them.

"That is right. Some said you healed with magic. Is that true?"

"No, it is not true. I cannot do any healing myself. Only God can do that. I can pray for people, and sometimes He heals them. Do you understand that?"

He nodded. "I think so. Will you ask God to heal my wife?"

Immediately I sensed this was something God wanted me to do. I said, "Okay."

My companions and I were very tired, and we still had much to do. Nevertheless, I said, "Yes, we will pray.

Take her down from the burro."

He did. We placed our hands on her, and she began to tremble. I took hold of her hand and said, "Get up! In the name of Jesus, get up!" And I helped her to her feet.

She grabbed hold of a fence and stood there, a look of surprise on her face. Her husband was speechless.

Later, while we were eating, the man joined us. His wife was mounted on the burro, but now she looked happy. When we had first seen her, she had looked very sad. And no wonder, her life had been difficult. All her housework had to be done while sitting down. She washed clothes while sitting down. She even cooked while sitting on the floor. Life had been very difficult and painful for her.

Now she was healed. No wonder she looked happy.

Her husband said, "I've come to ask you how much we owe you."

"How much you owe me?" I asked in astonishment. "For healing your wife? Are you sure she is healed?"

"*Sí, señor*," he said. "She is healed."

"How do you know she is healed?"

"Because she hasn't stood on her feet or walked for four years. Now she stands up, and she walks." The man was very moved.

I realized he wasn't a believer. So I told him, "What you owe me is to buy a Bible. You can buy one over there at the church. Then read your Bible every day. And go to that church ninety times. . . ."

"Buy a Bible? And go to church ninety times? That's all?

I do not pay you any money?"

"That's all," I said. I figured if he read his Bible every day and came to church a few times, he would come to know Jesus. And that's all the payment I wanted.

He started to go, then hesitated. "Some people say you heal with magic, and that it will go away soon."

I didn't answer.

"They say, 'Just wait for twenty-four hours. Then the magic power will go away, and she will be just the same as before!' "

"What do you say?"

"I don't know. You prayed in the name of Jesus. That doesn't sound like magic to me. But," he looked a little embarrassed, "but suppose something happens, and she can't walk anymore? What should I do?"

"Just do as I did," I told him. "Just put your hand on the spot that is weak or in pain and rebuke the pain or disease in the name of Jesus Christ, just as you saw me do."

A little doubtful, he nodded. "Okay, señor. I will remember."

The next morning his wife got up and swept the patio. Then she prepared breakfast and began doing the wash. He watched her very closely to be sure she was all right. When she appeared to be able to take care of herself, he went to the hills to care for his farm.

For years this man had suffered with a severe back condition. Sometimes the pain would become so strong that he would fall to the ground and be unable to get up. Others would have to come and get him.

During this particular day, the problem returned. The pain hit him suddenly. He slumped to the ground. He was all alone, miles from help. He thought, "What shall I do? There is nobody to help me."

Then he remembered what I'd told him about rebuking the pain. He gingerly placed his hand on the offending place in his back. And feeling a little foolish, he spoke out loud, "In the name of Jesus—in the name of Jesus—I rebuke the pain. In the name of Jesus, I command my back to be well."

Instantly the pain was gone, and he got up by himself and returned to work. He could hardly wait to finish his work that day. As soon as possible, he returned home to his wife. When he walked in the house, she was still on her feet, working. Apparently she'd been working hard all day long.

He asked, "How has it been with you today?"

She said, "*Muy bien!* Very well! Look at me. I have worked so hard that I have been sweating. And I still feel very fine. It's a miracle!"

He said, "Well, then this Sunday we're going to go over to the church. We'll attend services and buy a Bible."

Then he told her what had happened to him out in the field. Sunday they came and bought a Bible. True to his word, they began coming to church. Before long, they were saved. God began using this man in a remarkable healing ministry.

Now we realized that nearly all of the "signs following"

mentioned in the New Testament had been fulfilled. Only one remained, the promise of Jesus recorded in Mark 16:18 that said: ". . . if they drink any deadly thing, it shall not hurt them. . . ."

We thought this might refer to a child who would accidentally drink some deadly rat poison which we had in each of our homes to control the rodents. None of us dreamed the test would come to an adult—least of all, to myself. But such was the case.

In our travels we were in many homes. Sometimes I was alone, often with others. On this particular day, I was in a village of some people who were not very receptive to the Gospel. There were several of us together that time.

During the day, we got very thirsty. So we stopped at a hut and asked a woman to give us something to drink. She was not friendly, but agreed to satisfy our thirst. When she served us, as was our habit, we prayed. I prayed God's blessing upon the home. I thanked God for protecting us along the way. And I said, "Now, Lord, we thank You for this water. May Your blessing be upon it as we drink it. . . ."

When I drank, I noticed the water tasted very strange. And almost immediately I became very ill. "What's wrong, Victor?" one of my companions asked me.

"I don't know. But there must have been something in the water that disagreed with me. I must go outside. . . ."

I saw the woman watching me very carefully. I couldn't understand the look on her face. But she seemed to be pleased that I was ill. But right then I was so ill I hardly noticed.

When I got outside, I threw up, which was very unusual for me. But, as soon as I threw up, I was all right. We thanked the woman for her hospitality and went on our way.

Later we learned that the woman had put rat poison in my water. Apparently she had felt some resentment toward me for something she had heard me preach. God was good to me, because the rat poison we used in the jungle is so deadly that even a tiny bit of it on a piece of meat will quickly kill a dog or a human.

When we learned what she had done, we thanked God for His miraculous protection. We rejoiced in His care, and we prayed that this woman would come to know the Saviour.

Just before I went to sleep that night, I suddenly realized that God had just fulfilled the last of the five signs He promised would come to those who believe! And I could hardly sleep because I was so filled with praise.

Visions are something I have learned to treat with great respect. Dreams and visions both deserve respect, for that matter. God has revealed Himself and His plans for me, and for the church, through both.

One of the first times God spoke to me this way was shortly after I had moved to the farm outside Corozalito. Before going to sleep, I had been thinking about planting cacao, pineapples, coconut, and coffee. That was on my mind as I went to sleep, but it had absolutely no connection with my dream.

In the dream I was thinking about a number of communities that wanted to hear the Word of God. I thought, "I am going to go and preach to them."

I stood up, and I was all alone. I began walking, and before long I met several people. I didn't know them, but one young man joined me, and we went on together. After a while we came to a house. We knocked on the door, and I asked, "May we have a church service here?"

The people who lived there said, "Yes."

So we had a service which was very precious and full of joy. Then we left there to visit some very small villages where we had never been before. And then I woke up.

I thought, "I need to go to that place. Why else would God show me those villages, unless He wanted me to go to them?" I was willing to go. But I didn't know where these villages were, or the names of most of them. Even so, I was convinced that the people there wanted to hear the Word of God. Somehow I knew that I should go there.

I had some business to attend to, so I didn't go right away. After it was finished and I had the money in my hand, I came back to the church, where it was my turn to give the lesson.

I started talking about going out to give the message to those who are lost. Suddenly the message fell right back on top of me. I was telling others to go out and take the Gospel to them, but I had been more concerned about finishing my business deal and getting my money.

Why hadn't I used that money to make sure these people would hear the Gospel, or to care for the souls in my dream who were lost? While speaking, I began to cry and ask God to forgive me for my selfishness.

So I made plans to go. I didn't know the location of the place I had seen in my dreams, but I told God I would find it.

The first time I planned to go, my children became ill. So I didn't go. Finally they got well, and again I got ready. Once again, one of my children got sick. She was very, very ill, and it seemed that she might die.

I decided to go anyway. I told my wife, "She is a Christian. If she dies she will go to heaven. But those people who have never heard of Jesus, if they should die before I get there, where will they go?"

We both knew they would go to hell. So I had to go.

I told my neighbor I was going. "My little girl is sick," I said. "If she dies, please help my wife bury her. I will take care of the expenses when I return."

He said he would, but, thank God, it was not necessary, because she recovered rapidly.

Meanwhile I set out. By now the money I had received from the business transaction was gone. All I had in my pocket was two pesos. I started out as I had done in my dream, without anybody to go with me.

I told the Lord I would trust Him to show me who should go with me. I hadn't gone far when I met this young pastor named Juan. "Where are you going, Hermano Victor?" he asked.

"I don't know. I am going to a village named Iroso. But I don't know where that is."

He invited me to stay for the night. We had a church service that night, and the Lord blessed me very much. I prayed that God would guide and provide for me on the trip. But I didn't tell any details to anybody.

By six o'clock the next morning, I was ready to go. Just before I left the house, this young pastor showed up with his suitcase.

"Where are you going, Juan?" I asked.

"With you. I am going with you."

"You are?"

"Yes."

So I said, "Okay. Let's thank God for a good trip."

All I could remember in the dream was that the young man who was to go with me was tall and had light skin. This man fit the description. So after we gave thanks to God, we left. We traveled a long way through the jungle, all day long. There were no houses, no villages, absolutely nothing.

Late in the afternoon, we came to a house in a small clearing, and I recognized it. "Juan," I said, "this is the house I saw in my dream."

"Are you sure?"

"Yes, this is the place where we had a church service in my dream. We won't leave this place without having a service."

It was already getting dark when we arrived at the house. I knocked on the door. When the lady came, I said, "It is getting dark, and we don't know the road around here. May we stay for the night?"

She said, "Sure, no problem. Come on in."

"Thank you," I said. Then I remembered why we had come. I said, "If we are to stay here tonight, we will have a Gospel service."

"That's fine. That's good," she said, looking surprised.

"Have you ever heard of the Gospel?"

"I saw something in a dream, three nights ago."

This was an exciting confirmation. "Tell me about it."

She said, "Three nights ago I dreamed that a man with a book came to my house. People came in, many of them. They sang songs, songs of praise to God. I had never heard these songs before, but they were very nice. I liked them."

She pointed to the table. "And in the dream I had a pretty flower on my table, just like that one."

The woman told us that since having the dream, she had experienced an intense desire to know what the man with the book had to say.

"You've never heard the Gospel before?" I asked.

"No. I don't know what the word means. But if you will tell me, you may stay."

"That is why we have come."

Then I told her that God had shown me her house in a dream. I hadn't known where her village was but, with

God's guidance, had just started out. And He had led us here.

All her neighbors were invited. And in a little while twenty-four people crowded into the tiny house. I opened my Bible and told them about Jesus Christ and how to be saved.

Then I gave an invitation. Every person in the room raised his hand. I thought they hadn't understood me. I told them to put their hands down.

Once again I explained to them in detail what all this meant. "Now," I said, "whoever wishes to receive new life, please raise your hand." Again every hand was raised. Every person in that little house prayed and received Jesus Christ that night!

We sang and praised God till very late. They didn't want to let us go, so we promised to stay and have another service the following evening.

If possible, the next night was even better than the first. The people who had come the first time invited their neighbors. Ten new people came. Again I preached and gave an invitation. This time all the new people received Christ. We had another time of praise and rejoicing.

The name of the place is now called Nueva Esperanza. There is a healthy and prosperous church located there now. All this happened because of the vision God gave me in the dream.

Of the dreams and visions God has given me, I can't really consider any one of them as having been more important than another. However, there was one that came to me in 1972 about my brother Gregorio that changed his life in ways neither of us could have comprehended. And because of that, many, many others were affected in positive ways.

While I was praying one day, I saw my brother.

Someone was talking to him. I don't know who it was, but this person was inviting Gregorio to do something important, and the conversation seemed to involve a long trip.

Up till this time, Gregorio hadn't been out of the country. I had no idea what country the vision was suggesting. I mulled the whole thing over in my mind for quite a while before telling Gregorio.

Finally I told him.

He was surprised. "Victor, are you sure the invitation is to come to me?"

"Yes, I am sure. I asked the Lord to make it clear to me. Without a doubt, you are the one."

"How will the invitation come?"

"I don't know. Maybe someone will speak to you in person."

He was thoughtful. "And this invitation—you say it is very important? And that it might involve some travel?"

"Yes. It is very important. There will be much travel."

"What should I do about the invitation when it comes?" he asked. Obviously he believed in the authenticity of the vision, as I did.

"I believe you should accept it."

"Even if it means I must leave Colombia for a time?"

"Yes, all of that seemed clear to me."

We prayed together about the whole matter: the vision, our discussion, and all that it might mean. Then, for some time, perhaps two or three weeks, we didn't discuss it again.

Gregorio, meanwhile, was spending more of his time trying to help some of the lay pastors become more successful in the farming by which they earned their livelihood. For several years, Gregorio had been deeply concerned about the physical and social needs of our people. Since his conversion, he had always been concerned for their spiritual well-being. But this was something beyond that.

"We must do something more for our people than just preach to them," he told me one day.

"What do you mean?"

"Well, they are so ignorant, so backward in so many ways," he said. "We preach to them, and we should. But sometimes I have the feeling that we are failing them."

"Failing them?" I wasn't quite sure what Gregorio meant.

"Sometimes I feel almost hypocritical. I go to them and tell them Jesus loves them, and they can't really hear me." He looked troubled.

"Can't hear you?"

He shook his head. "No, they can't hear me when I'm talking about love and peace and forgiveness while their hungry bellies are growling. And it bothers me."

"But what can you do about it? What can any of us do about it?" I asked. "Hasn't it always been this way?"

"Yes, and that's part of the problem. Because it's always been this way, they don't even comprehend any possibility of change. They can't even think that it could be better, different some way from how it's always been."

I wasn't quite sure what he had in mind. But I said, "When we take the Gospel to the people, their lives are usually much better than they were before."

"I know that," he said. "When they quit spending most of their money on rum, then they begin to eat a little better. And then they sometimes learn to read and write. That helps them, too. But I am talking about something more than that."

"What is that?" I asked.

"I am thinking about helping them plant better crops and teaching them to make things they can sell to bring in cash so they can buy things they need, such as medicines and the right kind of food. . . ."

I agreed. "But our job is to preach, to tell them about a new life."

"A new life, Victor. That's just it. A new life can't come to them, not truly, till both their bodies and their souls become well."

All of these previous conversations with Gregorio came to me during the next days. "Perhaps," I thought, "perhaps this invitation, this trip, whatever it is, and wherever it takes my brother, will help him in beginning to fulfill his dream."

I don't remember exactly how long it was after Gregorio and I discussed my vision, but one day he came to me quite excited, waving a letter in his hand.

"Don David is coming!" he said. "David Howard is coming to Cartagena. And he has asked me to meet him there."

I wasn't surprised. "Perhaps this is part of the vision's fulfillment," I said. Soon after the letter came, Gregorio met with David for a couple of days. When he returned, he told me a most remarkable story.

Gregorio and I both knew that David Howard was living in the United States, working with Inter-Varsity Christian Fellowship. He was to be involved in Urbana '73, though neither of us knew very much about Urbana. Gregorio discovered it was a student missionary convention held by Inter-Varsity, every three years, at the University of Illinois, in Urbana.

Gregorio said, "David Howard asked me to speak at Urbana." Then he explained the purpose and extent of the meeting. "And they want me to be one of the main speakers! To speak to fifteen thousand students . . . !"

I gasped. "What can it mean . . . ?"

"I remembered what you told me, Victor," he said, "about the vision."

"Did you tell him you would come?"

Gregorio shook his head. "No. I told David I must first come and discuss the matter and pray about it with you."

What neither of us knew at that time was that God had also spoken to others about this matter. A short time before David Howard had come to Colombia to meet Gregorio, someone in Corozalito had spoken in tongues during a public meeting. There had been an interpretation that told of David's forthcoming trip, and he had been mentioned by name.

About the same time, someone in the Buen Pastor Church in Cartagena gave a message in tongues. The interpretation mentioned a Colombian who was soon going to be invited to the United States for a major ministry. Of course none of us knew anything about these happenings at the time.

Gregorio thought about the invitation for several weeks. We prayed about it, as did the church, and one day Gregorio said, "I believe God wants me to go."

I agreed.

"It scares me," he said. "I've never seen that many people at one time."

As it turned out, Gregorio did go to Urbana '73. And in ways that neither of us could have imagined, it changed his ministry.

10

Your Labor Is Not in Vain

Back in the first days, I had been quite ignorant of the ways of God. All of us were. There had been no one to guide us at that time. Later, missionaries like Bob Reed and David Howard came and advised us whenever we requested their help. But sometimes, in the beginning, we seemed to stumble around.

We really didn't stumble, though, because God was guiding us with His Holy Spirit. We realize that more now than we did then. Looking back from this point in time, we can now clearly see the method He used to teach us.

When I first came to Christ and began to work for Him, I was very much on fire, very zealous. I was eager to tell others what Jesus Christ had done in my life.

Though at first I had no systematic, carefully thought-out plan, God blessed my zeal. All I knew to do was to go and tell what I knew. As I did, God gave me more and more knowledge and faith, and I kept going out, sharing these new insights. Now I can see that God actually did give me a pattern, a plan.

God performed miracles. In nearly every village I visited, before I left, God had raised up a little group of believers.

Soon a congregation would come into existence. Then, before long, a church would be built.

David Howard once asked me to share my church-planting plan with him. Until then, I hadn't thought much about having such a "plan." But as we talked, it began to come into focus.

I told him, "When I first go to a village, I trust God to provide open hearts for His message. He always does that, and several people receive Jesus.

"I return to that place on a regular basis. And, each time, more people come to Christ. I remain in each place for quite a while to teach them from the Scriptures: how to live as believers and how to depend upon Jesus. I teach them these things very thoroughly."

He asked, "How many times do you visit a group like this before a church becomes established?"

"Five times, usually."

"Only five times?" he asked.

"Yes. Five visits are usually enough."

He was amazed. To me it seemed perfectly natural for us simply to serve as spokesmen for the Holy Spirit and to let Him take over. It never occurred to us that He would not do so. But according to David Howard this was not the normal experience of the missionaries. He said it was hard for them to learn to depend so completely on God and to be satisfied with following the Holy Spirit. Consequently, some work is done in the energy of the flesh, and results are much slower in coming.

I explained to him some of our methods for teaching the

Bible. One of the most effective is to sing the Scriptures. Colombians love to sing. And since we had no hymnbooks at first, and there are many churches without them even today, we began singing the Scriptures.

We sang long Scripture choruses, some of them telling entire Bible stories. Some of the songs would cover whole chapters. Somebody would compose the music, then everybody, children and adults alike, would learn the entire song, quickly.

Wherever they went, these new believers would sing.

You would hear farmers singing in the fields, men singing as they cut down trees, children singing as they played, and women singing as they worked in the garden or around the home.

In our church meetings, we always read a great deal of Scripture. And those who cannot read memorize many verses and chapters, simply by listening. Some people use their inability to read as an asset instead of a liability, even using it as a tool to witness.

One such man is Manuel Herrera. Even though he couldn't read, he carried his Bible with him.

When he met a friend who could read, he said, "You know I can't read, but I've got a book I'd like you to read to me."

When the unsuspecting friend took it, Manuel would say, "Find the part called the Gospel of John. Now find chapter three and read it to me."

After that chapter was read, Manuel would ask, "Do you understand what that was all about?"

"No, not completely."

"Well, let me tell you. . . ."

Then Manuel would begin his witness for Christ.

David and I spent many days together on the trail. We talked much about the Lord and the ways God was reaching the Colombians. He was often amazed at what I'd told him. Sometimes he said, "I find it hard to believe how effective your evangelism is."

There are a number of reasons for the effectiveness of our witness. One is that the people are so hungry for the Gospel that they listen and obey without question.

If any of them had had previous contact with a church, it had usually been just that: a church, not a living, vital, growing body. So when they are introduced to a Person—Jesus Christ, Himself—instead of to a church or dogma, they quickly respond.

These people had been so accustomed to the power of demons, witchcraft, and black magic that when they came face-to-face with a power that is superior, they were impressed and quickly responded. My brother Claudio is an example of that. His previous involvement in sorcery held no more attraction in the presence of the greater power of the Gospel of Jesus Christ. He told me he has never been sorry.

Another factor I can't overlook is that most people in our area of Colombia neither read nor write. So when someone brings a Bible into their home and teaches them to read from it, they simply begin walking in the light of the Word, as they read it. Their minds have not been cluttered with a lot of other stuff. So when they read or hear the Word, it falls on good ground, and they are easily converted.

I could hardly grasp what David told me. "The people in the United States and many other so-called civilized countries of the world are difficult to win to Jesus."

"Why?" I asked. "How can that be?"

He listed a number of reasons. One, that they had heard so much about Jesus Christ, heard so many sermons, seen so many churches, that they had lost interest.

"Are your churches in the United States growing quickly, like ours?" I asked.

David shook his head sadly. "Very few."

"I think I'd rather live down here, where people are eager to learn of a better life," I told him.

"Perhaps another reason our churches grow so fast," I told him, "is that we count it a privilege to become members. It is not easy to join our churches. We discipline ourselves very strictly.

"And when a brother sins, we talk to him, as the Bible says. If he repents, we accept him back into fellowship. If he does not, well, he cannot be a vital part of the church until he does."

I told David of the way we often prayed for a long time, waiting for God to give directions, before making decisions in the church.

"How do you do that—I mean make those decisions in your church meetings?" he asked. "By taking a vote?"

"No. We don't vote. We talk over every matter that comes up requiring a decision. We talk it out completely, then we pray. After that, we indicate, one by one, how we feel God has directed us individually. Almost always the matter is unanimous."

"What if it isn't unanimous?" David asked.

"Then we talk some more and pray some more, until we do come to a common agreement."

I told him that we also expect every member to share in the witnessing, in taking the Gospel to others. "We always go in groups or two by two," I said, "as Jesus sent them out."

"How do you select people to go out?" he asked me.

"We wait for the Holy Spirit to tell us who should go. And He often names the very people who should go out together.

"Training people to go out is a vital part of ministry. We accomplish this by taking a person with us a few times. We observe his conduct with others, the effectiveness of his witness, his familiarity with the Scriptures. When we feel he is ready, we allow him to preach."

David asked, "How can you know when he is ready?"

"You just know. Experience I suppose—with the Holy Spirit's guidance. He helps you to make the right decisions."

The proper exercising of spiritual gifts is a matter of extreme importance to us. At first there was much emphasis upon speaking in tongues, healing, and casting out demons. Later, through wise counsel and maturity, this changed.

Instead of allowing these more visible or dramatic gifts to predominate, we prefer to develop others, such as hospitality. Probably the most gifted person in this area is Maria de Amante, Calixto's wife. Naturally a warm, loving, and generous person, the welcome one receives in her home is emphasized by the love of Christ that flows from her.

David Howard, in particular, has commented on this woman's special gift. "Whenever I arrive at Calixto's home," he told me, "Maria always hands me a glass of thirst-quenching lemonade. Then she removes my trail-soiled shoes and socks, and washes and dries my feet. Through these loving acts, she brings to mind the way that Mary Magdalene cared for Jesus.

"Hers is a gift," David said, "a true gift of the Holy Spirit."

Other gifts that we seek to demonstrate are the gifts of love and prophecy, or preaching, sharing the Word of God.

We believe, as the Apostle Paul taught in 1 Corinthians, that all the gifts are important. But they are the Holy Spirit's gifts to us. And when He apportions them out to us, He does it correctly, in the right order and proportion, in ways that will benefit the whole Body of Christ.

We are seeking the gifts of God as He told us we should do. But even more, we are seeking to be filled and controlled by the Holy Spirit so that His love will naturally overflow into the lives of those who have not yet found Him.

As the churches had grown and prospered and we had reached out into the ripe harvest fields as far as possible, God began showing us new ways to minister. Claudio is now pastoring a growing congregation. His church at Santa Maria is prospering as new people come to Jesus regularly.

But God has led Gregorio and me in other directions.

We sensed this possibility a number of years ago, but made no move till it was clear we should do so. I had been aware of my own restlessness for some time, but I was not as aware of Gregorio's need for change. Not until he came to me that day, troubled in his spirit.

"Victor," he began, "we must begin doing more for our people."

"What more can we do?" I asked. "We are already bringing them to the Lord. We are helping them clean up their lives by teaching them to walk with Him. They are beginning to prosper."

"All of that is true," he broke in. "But they aren't really prospering as they should. Since they don't spend so much money on rum and beer as before, they have more for their families. They might eat better than before, but there is more. . . ."

"I'm not sure what you mean. Many believers are now learning to read and write. What more can we do for them?"

He crossed his legs and closed his eyes. "I'm not sure. But, Victor, many of them are still hungry."

"Haven't they always been?"

"That's true," he admitted. "But I don't think they have to go hungry, as hungry as that home I was in a few days ago."

Then he told me the story of how he had been invited to preach in a distant church. When he arrived, one of the families had arranged for Gregorio to stay with them. Just before the service time, the lady set the table for him. Though there were others in the home, Gregorio noticed only one plate on the table.

"What about the others?" he asked. "Have your children eaten?"

She said, "Don't worry about them. You eat." And she placed a single egg and some yucca on his plate. He bowed to pray. When he looked up, four small children were clustered around the table, their eyes hungrily glued on that egg.

He said, "Victor, I couldn't eat. I divided that egg four ways and gave it to the children. They gobbled it down as though they hadn't eaten in days."

Gregorio arose to go. "Victor, many farmers don't know how to raise proper crops. They grow the same thing year after year. When the land gets tired, they move to another place and do the same thing. They can't raise enough on their little places to make a living."

He was right, and I agreed. But I didn't know what to do about it and told him so.

"Neither do I," he said. "But I believe the Lord wants me to find ways to help them."

Many times after that he came and talked: about the bad water that made people sick, about the many children who died very young, about the mothers who died in childbirth, about hunger, malnutrition, tropical diseases. Gregorio would often weep as he described the needs to me. And I would weep with him.

I tried to console him. "Gregorio, it's not your job to do those things. You are a preacher, a pastor, an evangelist. Others are trained for that kind of ministry."

He shook his head. "I try to tell myself that, but God won't let me avoid the issue. Each time I talk to Him about it, He reminds me of the feeding of the five thousand."

"What do you mean?"

"Remember when the disciples came to Jesus and asked Him to send them away to get food? You know, to get help somewhere else. Do you remember what Jesus told them? 'You feed them. You take care of them.'

"So you see, Victor," he went on, "that's what's bothering me. Jesus is telling me to do these things. He's telling me to care for all those who are upon my heart."

Finally, Gregorio went to Dick Wolcott, then field administrator of the LAM in Colombia. Dick helped Gregorio think the whole plan through. And eventually he got started in the new ministry, doing what he felt God calling him to do. With Dick's help, Gregorio set up *Acción Unida* (United Action) to help mobilize the resources of the churches and to minister to their social needs. He enlisted volunteer physicians to go with missionary nurses to visit the remote villages which had never received any public-health services. There they cured the sick, pulled bad teeth, and taught hygiene and good nutrition.

At the same time, Gregorio would be preaching the Gospel and helping the visiting agronomist to show the farmers how to rotate crops, plant vegetables and fruit trees, and care for their animals.

My ministry has also drastically changed since those first years.

It was while I was still at Corozalito that I first recognized the needs of the Indians.

They lived deeper in the jungle than the towns we ordinarily visited, in places more inaccessible. I met the Domico brothers, who were Christians, and went with them to visit their people in Tierra Alta. I also heard about others who lived far to the west of us, near Panama. The culture and living conditions of these Indians were completely different from ours, as was their language. In fact, each Indian group in northern Colombia speaks a different language. This adds to the difficulty in reaching them.

Because of these problems, as well as their remoteness, nomadic habits, and desire to be left alone, very little evangelistic work was being done among the Choco Indians, sometimes referred to as the Epera Indians.

At first I did some witnessing and preaching among the Chocos. They were not nearly as easy to work with as my own people. But as I spent time among them, they began to know me, to accept me, and really to listen to me.

Still it was a long time before I was able to see any results.

I despaired of having any converts when I had been there several years without seeing any receive Christ. I complained to the Lord about it.

"You helped me reach so many before," I told Him. "And now I don't seem to be doing any good. Shall I quit and go back to my own people?"

As He had done once before in my ministry, at another time when I was about ready to quit, God directed me to His Word.

I read once more:

> Therefore, my beloved brethren, be ye stedfast, unmoveable, always abounding in the work of the Lord, forasmuch as you know that your labour is not in vain in the Lord.
>
> 1 Corinthians 15:58

"Thank You, Lord," I said. "Thanks for reminding me again."

I did as He directed, and one by one over thirty Indians in one tribe came to know the Lord! I knew it was a tremendous victory. Then God sent to me the help I had prayed for: a younger man, one who could learn the language and customs better than I. His name is Jose Moreno, a very spiritual, talented man.

Work among the Indians is so slow, so difficult. In Corozalito I would simply tell people about Jesus Christ, and they would eagerly accept Him. Then, when the Holy Spirit was poured out upon the church, thousands came to Christ.

It was not the same among the Indians.

I am working just as hard now as before, maybe even harder. I am learning to lean more and more upon God. I am praying for an outpouring of the Holy Spirit upon the Indians, as we had in Corozalito.

11

United With Jesus

Recently I have been traveling more extensively in the northern part of Colombia, and I have been excited to see how the Gospel has spread. There are at least two hundred organized congregations in our Association of Evangelical Churches of the Caribbean; and I have visited the majority of them, because I am a licensed evangelist.

But when I first began to serve the Lord, I found myself in a very strange situation. Though God was blessing my efforts in bringing many people to Jesus and forming and nurturing many congregations and churches, there was a sadness in me.

I could not become a member of a church myself, neither could I be baptized, or partake of the Lord's Supper. For many reasons this did not seem fair, because many of those who were able to share in these blessings were people I had personally introduced to this new life.

I can understand the reasoning behind part of this. But I could not clear up the matter because of the governmental red tape involved. I was not the only one to be denied these privileges. My good friend and Christian brother, Alfredo, suffered with me, as did others.

Most of this had to do with our marital relationships.

Alfredo Acevedo had been married many years ago, long before he became a Christian. He and his wife were childless, and for various reasons they decided to separate. This became a problem: Since divorce was not possible in Colombia, they were still legally married.

Alfredo began living with another woman, whom he could not marry, and to them were born three children. After a while he left this woman and took a third one. By this woman he also had three children.

Alfredo and the third woman became Christians and began raising their children in a Christian home.

Now the question: To whom was Alfredo, now a Christian, responsible?

Some older Christians told him he must leave his Christian mate and family and return to his legal wife. In agony of spirit, Alfredo tried to do this, but she wouldn't have him. This left Alfredo with an incredible mess on his hands.

Alfredo's only hope was for his legal wife to die. Then, and only then, would he be free to remarry.

Because of this situation, Alfredo and others with similar problems were not allowed to join the church, to teach publicly, be baptized, or receive the Lord's Supper.

Despite this, Alfredo was one of the finest examples of a changed man in the whole Corozalito area. He was very aggressive in his witness and led many people to Christ. Through it all, Alfredo maintained a Christlike attitude. But sometimes he got discouraged and would come to me. We would talk about it and pray.

Then he would smile. "Christ suffered much more than I am suffering."

Since my own situation was so close to his, I could only agree. However, mine was different. I had not been married to any of the three women I had lived with. My problem had to do with governmental restrictions and the slow-moving civil courts.

For you see, in Colombia the government would not recognize a Protestant wedding. We had to be married by a civil judge. Only then could evangelical Christians have a church wedding.

For years I had tried again and again to cut through all this red tape. But the wheels of the courts had ground so slowly that I had not as yet succeeded.

Time and again I would be present as new believers were baptized. I saw the joy on their faces. And I longed to be one of the candidates. I would even welcome them into the church as new members. Yet I, the one who had first told them about Jesus and had prayed with them as they opened their hearts to Him, I could not become a member of the church and partake of these blessings.

Many times I have sat in the back of the church and wept as David Howard and others served the Lord's Supper. How I wished I could receive the elements of Jesus' broken body and His poured-out blood. But I could not.

David would often ask, "Victor, do you have the red tape straightened out yet, so you can be married?"

"No," I told him again and again.

"Will you let me know when it happens?"

"You will be notified immediately!" And I would say to him as I had before, "Teresa and I want you to marry us, baptize us, and accept us into church membership. Will you do that, Don David?"

"I would be very honored, and I would then like to be the first to serve the Lord's Supper to you."

Finally the day came. I received my notification that all was in order. I could finally be married. I sent word to David. He responded, saying, "I will come to Corozalito for Easter week. We will then go to Montelibano."

I was like a little boy. I counted the days, even the hours. Finally Easter came. As much as I always enjoy Easter, this time my mind was on the days *after* this great event. A couple of days after Easter, David and Teresa and I, along with several others from Corozalito, started out.

My heart was light, and I was praising God all the way. We reached the San Jorge River, engaged the Jonson canoe, and started downriver. As we rounded a bend in the river, we met another Jonson going upriver. I recognized one of the men on board.

"Look, David. Look! That's the judge! He's the one who is supposed to marry us."

David tried to encourage me. "Maybe he'll be back, or maybe there's another judge in Montelibano."

I was heartsick, because I was afraid that once again I had missed my chance.

In the county-seat building in Montelibano, we met another municipal judge. I told him the situation. "Will you perform the ceremony?" I asked.

He said, "Yes, but not today. Come back tomorrow."

Even though I knew this was the typical Colombian *mañana* way, "do it tomorrow," I was disappointed. I had waited so long.

"Can't you do it today?" I pleaded. "We have come a long way."

He shook his head. *"Vengase mañana.* Come back tomorrow and we will do it."

David was impatient, too. He said, "Sir, this man has waited a very long time. Now he has traveled two days to get here. And I have come all the way from Cartagena to witness the event. We would really appreciate it if you would be willing to marry them today."

The judge was firm. "Come back tomorrow. We will do it then."

But David was insistent. After some pressure, the judge said, "Well, come back at five o'clock. It's one o'clock now. Come back in four hours."

"We will be here, sir," I told the judge, hoping he would remember and be there himself.

That afternoon we found a good place for the baptism. The news spread throughout the community, "Victor Landero will be married today! Then he will be baptized!"

I was anxious and nervous. I was eager to be legally married to Teresa, the mother of my children. And I wanted to become a complete part of the Church in every way. So five o'clock could not come fast enough.

We were at the courthouse early. And the judge was there, as he had promised. The ceremony was brief, but we didn't care. For us the true wedding would take place later.

From the courthouse we immediately went to the church for the ceremony I had so long awaited. I was proud of my family: Teresa and our five children. All of them were there.

While I impatiently waited for everything to be ready, I looked myself over. I had changed into my clean shirt and khaki pants. My sneakers were worn, but clean. In the back, Teresa sat nursing our youngest child. The church had furnished her with a new cotton dress.

"Thank You, God," I said. "I am so grateful for Your goodness."

The wedding was not long, but it was very meaningful, very moving for all of us. David pronounced us husband and wife, and I looked at my bride. We had come a long road together. I was so thankful to God for her.

I paused for a brief moment of reflection. Then I said to David, "I am now ready to be baptized." To the Lord I whispered, "I've been ready for a long, long time."

The whole congregation from the Montelibano church was there, as they had been at the wedding. I was glad. But somehow it didn't matter if anybody was there. Jesus was there, and I was there. And I had come to enter the waters of baptism with Him, my Lord. I was soon to rise in newness of life with Him.

I was so happy, so blessed.

Every part of that sacrament is still very vivid in my mind.

We stood on the bank and read Scripture. Then we sang

some hymns. I hardly remember anybody else being there except my Lord. It almost seemed that I was transported into Jesus' very presence. I was so eager to be baptized. Yet I didn't want it to be over. I had anticipated this for so long; I wanted to enjoy every precious moment.

David reached for my hand and led me down into the water. There we stood and sang another hymn. I could almost see heaven opening up. I could almost hear God speaking to us.

David said, "Now we are ready."

I said, "Please, let's sing the hymn again."

So we did.

I had to pray. My heart was so full. "Oh, Jesus, my Jesus, the time has come for me to be baptized, as You were—for me to join myself to You in Your death and resurrection—for me to show to the world that I have been cleansed of my sins by Your grace and mercy. Can this privilege be mine, who am so unworthy, by faith? Thank You, thank You." David told me afterwards that he had been very moved as I lifted my hands to heaven and talked with Jesus.

I don't know how long I talked with Him. To me it seemed as but a moment. But the sun was going down when I said, "David, Don David, now I am ready."

I can't possibly describe how I felt when I was immersed, and when I was raised from the waters as my Jesus had been raised from the dead. I won't try to tell you. But it was wonderful.

Then we went back to the church for the Lord's Supper. It was so good, so good, for all this to happen to me on a single day. It seemed as if I couldn't take any more blessing. Yet I opened my heart to more of Jesus' love and presence. And somehow He filled it full again and again.

As David passed the broken bread to me, I wept. "This is Jesus' body," I said. "And it was broken for me. Oh, thank You, Jesus!"

As I drank the wine, "Jesus, this is Your blood, that You shed for me. Thank You, thank You."

In some wonderful way, I had become united with Jesus. I had become one with Him. I had been His before today. But I knew that in a different way than I could comprehend, I now belonged to Jesus Christ in such a way that nothing could ever take me from His side.

David Howard embraced me. "Victor," he said, and I was astonished to see that he was weeping too, "this has been the most blessed day of my life."

I couldn't speak. I could only nod and clasp my brother close to my heart. Never again will my life be the same.

Epilogue

The Work Continues

After working with the Chocos for a number of years, Victor moved to Gilgal, a tiny village near the Colombia-Panama border. There, since 1974, he has been evangelizing the Cuna Indians. It was there, at Gilgal, in his comfortable, thatched hut in the jungle, that I met Victor Landero: legend in his own time.

One could not have found a more humble man. We talked, seated on rawhide-backed chairs in his patio, as pigs, chickens, dogs, turkeys, children, parakeets, and Indians wandered in and out. It was a day I shall long remember.

Though Victor is not a large man, I felt as if I was seated in the shadow of a giant. Speaking of the work of the Holy Spirit, Victor rarely raised his voice. But now and again I detected a sparkle in his eye as he described how God had ". . . chosen the foolish things of the world to confound the wise . . . and the weak things of the world to confound the . . . mighty" (1 Corinthians 1:27).

Since I spoke no Spanish and Victor no English, Shirley Jamieson, a nurse of the Latin America Mission, translated both my questions and his answers: a cumbersome method for an interview.

Yet God broke down the barriers—first through David Howard, now through myself—and brought us together as brothers.

He informed us that God was breaking through to the Cuna Indians, although not to the degree He had to the people at Corozalito. "Not yet," he said. "But I am praying for that day. And already nine Cunas have come to Christ. That's a victory!"

Though Victor is sponsored by the Association of Evangelical Churches of the Caribbean, he uses much of this salary to pay teachers to come to the local village. As he has done for years, Victor trusts God for his daily bread.

I also met with Gregorio, who shared with me the realization of his dreams to help his people. He administers Acción Unida, his bold plan for attacking ignorance, poor health, and poverty.

Through this ministry Acción Unida, working closely with the churches, treats the sick, provides dental care, assists in community development, helps develop handcrafts, and teaches good farming techniques to struggling farmers. Christians who have been suffering from poverty, malnutrition, and psychological defeat have been given new hope. All of this, as well as becoming a stronger witness to their neighbors.

I spent time with Victor, Gregorio, and Claudio, three of the legendary Landero brothers, and with Juan Gonzales and Franco Bohorquez—all of them mightily used of God, both then and now.

After we had shared and talked together for several days,

Gregorio said, "I will read some Scripture before we part." He read, "Bless the Lord, O my soul: and all that is within me, bless his holy name . . ." (Psalms 103:1). Then we knelt to pray.

And how those men spoke with God. They know Him on a personal, intimate basis. They addressed Him in humility and with deep faith, their praise genuine, their expectation sincere.

"No wonder God chose them," I thought, "and the place where they dwelt, to enrich thousands by reaching them with His mighty power."

But it wasn't because of who they were that God used them. It was because of God's call and sovereign power that they became the spiritual giants that they are.

He is truly the One, I thought, *who gives the increase.*

BOB OWEN